# REFLECTIONS
## ON THE
# MODERN
## AND THE
# GLOBAL

# REFLECTIONS
## ON THE
# MODERN
## AND THE
# GLOBAL

# BRUCE MAZLISH

**Transaction Publishers**
New Brunswick (U.S.A.) and London (U.K.)

This book is printed on acid-free paper that meets the American National Standard for Permanence of Paper for Printed Library Materials.

Library of Congress Catalog Number: 2013000656
ISBN: 978-1-4128-5184-8
Printed in the United States of America

Library of Congress Cataloging-in-Publication Data

Mazlish, Bruce, 1923-
  Reflections on the modern and the global / Bruce Mazlish.
    pages cm
  ISBN 978-1-4128-5184-8
  1. Civilization, Modern. 2. Globalization. I. Title.
  CB357.M42 2013
  909--dc23
                                                                2013000656

I dedicate this book to my grandchildren, Zachary, Dean, Eve, Jacob, and Caleb, and hope that the world in which they will be living will be a humane one, fit for all of Humanity.

# Contents

# Acknowledgements

Much of my indebtedness to other historians and social sciences will be seen from my footnotes in the book. In addition, I would like to acknowledge the special assistance and support given me in the writing of this volume by Neva Goodwin, Annette Visbeck, and Kenneth Weisbrode. Each will now the reasons for my recognizing her or him. I would also like to thank Mary E. Curtis and Hannah K. Jones of Transaction Publishers for their encouragement and assistance in the course of my writing this book.

# Introduction

Over the past five hundred years or so, historians and other social scientists have perceived and constructed an extraordinary happening. It is the transition from the so-called Middle Ages via the Renaissance to modernity. Dating is essential to the historian's craft. In any case, we need to inquire into the nature of that modernity in order to understand ourselves today. It is also imperative that we understand that a comparable transition has been taking place in the last fifty years or so, from modernity to globalization, and equally imperative that we try to understand globalization and its vicissitudes.

Both developments—modernity and globalization—have proceeded unevenly in different parts of the world and with different timing. Developments that can be grouped under the heading of modernity have moved through various stages, such as the eighteenth-century Enlightenment, again at different paces and with different results. Everywhere, starting with Western Europe where it originated, modernity has triggered antimodern movements of thought and action. We can expect no less with globalization.

Thus our task is a difficult one. Within our analyses we must always keep complexity in mind, without it paralyzing us. We must always try to be aware of nuances. Scholarship on our subjects is enormous, much of it excellent, and again we must try to be informed by it without drowning in its cross-currents.

Let us take the plunge. First, however, a few preliminary muscle stretches. It is essential to realize that modernity must not be confused with modernization or modernism. Modernization is a process whereby the material trappings of modernity, its science, technology, and business methods, are taken up by a previously non-modern country. It is often preceded by two of the less admirable features of modernity: imperialism and colonialism. The malignity of these two features can perhaps be mitigated by the argument that they have existed for eons, in all kinds of forms, and may have been at their most benevolent in various places under modernity—but also at their most hideous.

As for modernism, it was a phase of modernity, manifested mostly in the arts and literature, which turned against realism. It need not figure further in our inquiry, except to note that it was spoken of as an international movement (which meant mainly European).

Of much greater importance was (and is) the existence of antimodernity at every moment of modernity. Present at the creation, as Chapter 1 will show, it has persisted at every step of the way until today. Strong antimodernity feeling and thought has made itself manifest especially in fundamentalist movements of various sorts.

Modernity has been strongly marked by its insistence on freedom of political and religious dissent and the rights of man (later expanded to include women, i.e., all humans). It did not happen all at once, but as a gradual development. Landmarks are the Glorious Revolution of 1688–89, and its confirmation of an elected parliament's having the right to participate in the country's governance; the Declaration of Man and the Citizen at the time of the French Revolution of 1789; and the gradual extension of suffrage in both England and France. The culmination of this movement can be seen in the era of globalization with the UN Declaration of Human Rights in 1948.

It should be clear that I do not view modernity as an essence, though it may have certain essential features, but as a dynamic, changing development. Indeed, its emphasis on the new and a demand for the ever new again is a clear indication that it should not be seen as an essence.

(2)

My approach will be in terms of reflections rather than seeking to add to the enormous amount of archival research that already exists. I use the term *reflections* for what follows, in the same manner as Edmund Burke did in his *Reflections on the Revolution in France* (1790). He was trying to make sense of what was happening in 1789, not trying to write a history of the event (as Thomas Carlyle did later). I am attempting to do the same in regard to thinking about the modern and the global, and the transition between the two. In this case, the subject is a process, not a momentous event.

What follows this short introduction are a number of what could be called essays, in the sense of *attempts*. I prefer to use the term *reflections*, as reflecting the fact that I am building on research, thinking, and writing undertaken during the course of the last few decades. One can contemplate the transition from the modern to the global as a continuous, seamless development, or emphasize it as a break or a rupture. I favor the latter view as offering us greater understanding. Indeed, one of the chapters is devoted to exactly this argument.

In the spirit described above, I have chosen to look at modernity by putting a few slices of it, so to speak, under a microscope. First, there is a chapter giving a short history of the phenomenon, to serve as a context for what follows. The arising conflict took place under the heading of "The Battle of the Ancients and the Moderns." It was fought on numerous terrains: literature, religion, and science. Charles Perrault, for example, fought it mainly in regard to literature, which in fact was mainly a losing field. Jonathan Swift, in turn, fought it on the grounds of technology and science, where he won the battle but lost the war.

Next, I examine three essential features: what I call the "seeing revolution," the notion of self (concomitantly involving a notion of society), and capitalism. The seeing revolution is the story of Copernicus, Kepler, and Galileo, of the emergence of linear perspective, and of new instruments, such as the telescope and microscope. It also implied and sometimes acted out a conflict between religion and science. In any case, the revolution entailed a new way of seeing that extended everywhere. The larger rubric has been called the scientific revolution of the seventeenth century.

In the chapter on the Self, I argue that the seeing revolution was accompanied by a changed notion of what it meant to be a self: a self that inhabits a scientific world. Unlike the seeing revolution, this development did not occur everywhere. It was a long, slow process by which the self became self-conscious. Key intellectual figures along the way were Descartes, Adam Smith, and Hegel. Individualism becomes a motif, and finds expression both in romanticism and classicism. It also smacks of Eurocentrism.

The last slice of modernity that I try to look at is related to capitalism. There has been capital almost from the beginning of humankind's emergence. A *capitalist society* is something new. This requires us to realize that the very notion of society—the reification of the idea—in other words, the consciousness of a group of people within which the individual comes to find his/her self must slowly emerge. Only then can we place capitalism in its modern setting.

(3)

First and foremost, the modern is a form of historical periodization. It emerges in Europe at the time of the

Renaissance, when the classics of Greek and Latin antiquity are revived, and is intended to mark their boundaries, with something called the Middle Ages in between. Later historians have played with numerous variations on the idea, writing about early and late modernity, and the same in regard to the medieval period. At the other end, in contemporary times, some have spoken of postmodernity. This has had a short shelf life, being superseded by globalization.

More lasting has been the association of modernity with the ceaselessly new, the ever-changing nature of a supposedly autonomous individual. At its heart is a rejection of tradition, with even earlier manifestations of modernity being regarded as new traditions. There is also an explicit or implicit connection to a belief in popular participation in the political process, in various human rights such as freedom of religion, freedom of popular demonstrations, and freedom of speech and press. This attitude of mind persists into the globalization process of today.

It must be noted that modernity has a pejorative side. It has been used to justify imperialism, the imposition of Western rule over non-modern peoples. It is the white man's burden to bring the perceived benefits of modernity to lesser societies. In this task, it is similar to the notion of *civilization*. Here, too, the barbarians must be conquered in order to bring them into civilized society. This misuse should not disqualify the importance of modernity, any more than the misuse of the term *democracy* should require us to discredit the entire idea.

In this introduction I wish to stress a few additional features of the subject. The first is that modernity must be distinguished sharply from modernization. Modernity concerns an attitude. This attitude is historically linked with the scientific revolution of the seventeenth century, and philosophically with the spirit of free and continuous inquiry. This, in turn, is connected to a way of seeing, with an emphasis on perspective. It is also tied to a sense of the self as an autonomous, self-creating being in a society made by it and other selves, and not by god. Modernization, on the other hand, is the transportation of the material aspects of modernity into one's own and into other societies.

Next a few further comments in regard to modernity and its tie to capitalism. Modern society has been spread by the economic forces under capitalism. As Karl Marx for one so perceptively remarked, it was bourgeois capitalism that irresistibly created a world market. This expansion has helped bring into existence the modern processes of globalization. These processes can be seen as a continuation of modernity, a supplement to it, or a supplanting of it. As I have already remarked, I think we gain great understanding of globalization by looking at it as a rupture.

Looked at this way, we can examine the way globalization requires new categories of thinking. The most glaring example is in regard to the nation-state. It will not disappear but is being changed in nature; this is already happening. Many of the challenges with which human beings now have to deal are global, as with the now recognized problems of climate change and ecological exhaustion. Their solutions require a transcendence of the nation-state, not its disappearance.

In the attempt at the required global solutions, I argue for the vital necessity of a concept of Humanity. My discussion of this concept will be found in two of the chapters in this book (and earlier in my book *The Idea of Humanity in a Global Era*, 2009). As can be seen, I am not writing a traditional history of the topic; rather I am reflecting on some key aspects of this most important transition in the history of the human species. My perspective, needless to say, is an evolutionary one, and one in which past, present, and future intertwine in our practice of history.

Returning to the seventeenth century, we note the decisive split between the divine and the secular as dominant explanatory devices, as mirrored in all subsequent historiography. It is not that individual scientists might not be deeply religious—the so-called battle of science and religion may have been true in principle, but not in its principals—but that prior to the seventeenth and eighteenth centuries in Western minds it was religion that was the measure of development, and now it was science.

(4)

Globalization, I am arguing, marks a transition beyond modernity. The chapters on globalization in this book are attempts to indicate some of the process, or processes, of the subject. In the first of these chapters, I make the argument that post–World War II developments are best understood in terms of a rupture. Defining globalization as increased interdependence and interconnectivity, accompanied by further compression of time and space, we see the process accelerated by the computer revolution and launching of artificial satellites. I then apply this analysis to the events of 1989, placing them in the framework of globalization. Next, although global history is supposed to transcend national boundaries, I show that in fact it all too often is made to serve national purposes.

Globalization, in my view, does not only have economic consequences, but perhaps even more importantly fosters a new kind of consciousness. I speak here of the concept of Humanity. An idea/ideal held by philosophers such as Kant, it now comes down from the heavens and manifests itself in reality. Thus, in one chapter I describe the movement from the sentiment of humanity to the concept itself. I enlarge the idea in my penultimate chapter, placing it in the overall context of social bonding as extended by globalization.

Only after these chapters, giving us a better idea of the nature of the subject, will an attempt be made at a conclusion. In that final chapter, I shall inquire further into the nature of the transition from modernity to globalization and its consequences. The reader is now invited to take a flight into the space and time that surrounds us.

# 1

# A Short History of Modernity

The term *modernity* goes back to the fifth century AD and the time of the Roman Empire, or rather its so-called decline and fall (in fact, of course, it persisted vigorously in the East). This linguistic innovation—*moderni* in contrast to *antique*—became a marker of importance, whose true content was to be realized later, well after its birth. What was immediately important was the term's creation of the ancient, against which the modern could begin to define itself. In fact, of course, what followed after the fifth century was what came to be called the Middle Ages, allowing for the ancient and the modern to pull apart.[1]

Thus, as we try to define modernity, it is necessary to recognize that it is from its inception a form of periodization. Although not really codified until the Renaissance, the tripartite division into ancient, medieval, and modern is implicit in its original coinage. Thereafter there are many modifications. Historians speak of early modernity as well as of late modernity; and of course they write about low and high middle ages. What is constant is the attempt to make sense of the past by classifying it into particular periods of time, which each then takes on a life of its own. The periodization can even become an agent, as when we speak of modernity as causing something.

All this is well known, though one often needs a reminder. The literal meaning of modernity is "just now." It is always, therefore, by definition new. Implicitly, there can be no stasis, no unchanging essence to modernity, unless we consider change and newness as its essence. As one author recently put it, modernity is a "condition of existence whose major feature is acceptance of historical change." Its adherents, we are told, have a sense of "living in the future."[2] Theirs is a new consciousness. In short, modernity is a constantly new and unfolding attitude, defining itself in the course of historical experience, which immediately then goes beyond its own momentary definition as a result of new experience.

Modernity is a social construction, a category by which to view the world and in terms of that view to remake it. To repeat: modernity is not an abstraction, a timeless entity, but an attitude that manifests itself in historical terms. For this reason we must now go beyond the kinds of general statements that I have been making. For most of this book, therefore, I will be engaged with the details of how in key episodes modernity has emerged in the history of the human species. I will not be writing a history of this emergence as such, but rather focusing on crucial features of its development.

Consequently, I will first take up a quintessential episode, the so-called battle of the ancients and the moderns, in the remainder of this present chapter. This encounter in the late seventeenth century marks the full-scale awareness of what is at stake. It will introduce us to our subject.

Then, rather than continuing with a formal history of modernity, its various multiples over time, for example, as a seventeenth-century version that then gives way to variants such as an Enlightenment followed by an industrial modernity—all being holistic constructions made up of the constellation of elements that contemporaries and we ourselves figure out as characteristic of the phenomenon—I will focus on central aspects of the experience. One example is what I will be calling the seeing revolution. Another is the view of the Self. And so on.

In this way, I will try to suggest what is involved in *any* modernity in terms of a sub-stratum of a developing consciousness and sub-consciousness. Once this is accomplished, I will then turn to globalization, seeking to understand it both as a continuation of modernity and in its own terms. Finally, I will undertake a comparison of modernity and globalization as categories of thought by which we seek to understand and try to order our existence.

## (2)

In 1687, Charles Perrault wrote a long poem, *Le Siècle de Louis le Grand*, immediately followed at the end of the year by *Parallèle des Anciens et des Modernes*, with three revised editions between 1688 and 1696–7. These works were the opening salvos in what came to be called the quarrel, or the battle, or the parallel of the ancients and the moderns. Though today most famous for his *Tales of Mother Goose*, the French author only came to the *Tales* toward the end of his life. Before that, in addition to his writings such as listed above, he had been involved in the creation of the Academy of Sciences, the restoration of the Academy of Painting, and the founding of the Academy of Inscriptions and Belles Lettres, of which he was made secretary for life. Clearly a man of many parts, in his defense of modernity, or actually his offense in its name, Perrault was equipped to fight on many fronts.

He was not without precedents. In 1670, Jean Desmarets de Saint-Sorlin published his *Comparaison de la langue et de la poésie française avec la grecque et la latine*, which affirmed, as one commentator puts it, "that antiquity had already reached an unsurpassable degree of perfection," first given it at the moment of creation.[3] However, what was missing was invention, which allowed artists to do more than just imitate nature. This, of course, meant that the modern could add something new—an assertion that was itself breathtakingly new in its self-assertion.

In his own writings, Perrault claimed that French literature was superior to Greek and Latin literature. This claim was tied from the beginning to praise of his own time and of his king, Louis XIV. For Perrault, great literary accomplishments are built upon the existence of a great monarch and a great nation. In his *Le Siècle de Louis le Grand* this note is sounded loud and clear. Thus, Perrault was not only attacking the worship of the ancients, but extolling the power and prestige of the French king. From the beginning, then, the struggle was laden with political meaning.

That meaning, however, is complicated in this early expression of modernity. In speaking of a "century," Perrault is abandoning the usual dynastic history, and appealing, instead, to the calculating spirit of his time. A century is a hundred years, and acquires a character separate from that even of the king. It has the same impersonality as a meter or other mathematical measurements. It implies that it will be succeeded by other centuries. Thus, the spirit of change is built into this new periodization. It indicates clearly that much time—centuries—has passed since the ancients. On this awareness a sense of superiority can be based.

The irony is that first the ancients had to be rediscovered and reestablished in all their glory. This was the task of the Renaissance, when antiquity was reborn. Only when the greatness and purity of the ancients had been recovered could moderns such as Perrault go on to surpass them. The literature of the ancients had embodied the universal and the unchanging. Now the moderns in their literature, recognizing a worthy antagonist, could argue that in the seventeenth century originality and genius had given birth to something superior to their predecessors. Individual judgment was now valued and brought into play, as the literary innovator proceeded according to his "own lights," a wonderful forecasting by Perrault of the Enlightenment to come.[4]

In the *Parallèle*, Perrault coupled advances in technology to those in regard to literature. Building on Desmarets de Saint-Sorlin's distinction between imitation and invention, Perrault praised the moderns' use of the latter as progressing beyond the work of the ancients. The example he offered was that of a mechanical device for fabricating silk stockings. Replacing the skilled workman whose output was distinctly limited, Perrault wrote about the machine: "How many little springs draw the silk fibers toward them, then let them go and take them up again & pull through such-and-such a stitch in an inexplicable fashion, & all this while the laborer who operates the machine understands nothing, knows nothing, nor even thinks about it."[5]

Perrault's point was that the ancients did not know of such a machine. We, in hindsight and foresight, can see that Perrault was anticipating Adam Smith and his description of pin manufacturing, the famous example he used in *The Wealth of Nations* to help explain the division of labor characterizing the new commercial and industrial society. Both men, Perrault and Smith, are also aware that one price for such modernity is dull-witted workers who do not understand the process in which they are engaged. Smith, of course, differs from the author of the *Parallèle* by having a clear insight into the "inexplicable fashion" by which the machine works. As we also know, this insight was given powerful visual as well as literary representation in the *Encyclopedia* of the eighteenth century.

With these brief remarks on parts of the contents of Perrault's writings, I want to step back and make some general remarks about the quarrel taking place. In back of this expression of it, with the term modernity vigorously entering the public domain, we can see previous expressions of the problem. Foremost in the struggle was Francis Bacon, who waged what we now identify as the battle against the ancients, whom he attacked under the label tradition. Without rehearsing his work, we can recognize his trumpeting of modern science—he didn't use the term modern—over that of the past. He urged his contemporaries to see for themselves, looking at the actual phenomena, rather than seeking truth in the texts of the ancients.

With such "Advancement of Learning" in mind, Bacon also argued for a different perspective on time. We, not those of past times, are the older, and are gifted with greater knowledge and mechanical genius because of that longer experience. The so-called ancients are, in fact, the children of the race, whereas we are the grown-ups. We have science well beyond that of our ancestors, and by following certain rules for acquiring further knowledge—the accumulation of empirical and experimental work—we can expect to expand our advantage.

In an entirely different modulation, but in the same key, was the voice of René Descartes. Capturing the sense of universality and unity from the ancients and their classics, the French scientist placed that sense in a secular science based on reason. In godlike tones, Descartes argued that by his mind alone, freed from the dross of actual experience, he could construct the universe exactly as God had done. There is no need to rehearse the details of Descartes's philosophy, which is well known. Here I want only to emphasize how, in an opposite fashion from Bacon, the author of the *Discourse on Method* preached the same message: there was nothing in the past or the ancients that we couldn't do as well and better.

With Perrault, the terrain of battle is shifted to literature. It is culture rather than science that gives the palm to the modern (although the scientific in the form of technology is hinted at). As early as the beginning of the seventeenth century—the OED claims 1635 for the first usage; an arbitrary citation I suspect—the term *modernity* in English is in existence. It reflects the work of writers such as Bacon and Descartes, with their path-breaking assertion of the superiority of present times to those of antiquity. By the end of the century, with Perrault and others like him, the term has taken on a self-reflexivity and a centrality that it had previously not enjoyed. The *Parallèle* stands for a symbolic shift, one in which the battle is openly joined and a flag sturdily planted. Henceforth for the next three hundred years or so, modernity stands triumphant.

(3)

From the very beginning, of course, there was opposition. In fact, most contemporaries would have thought that the victory belonged to the ancients. Tradition, they would have thought, had emerged triumphant from the contest. Perrault's opponents, such as Boileau, seemed to have won the contest. In condemning the new literary genre, the novel, which had not existed in antiquity, the traditionalists were also condemning all that was new. There were others on Perrault's side—foremost among them perhaps being Fontenelle, whose *Digression sur les anciens et les modernes* also appeared in 1688—but not unexpectedly the old order had more adherents than the new lights.

Yet the future lay with Perrault and his associates. They were creating a public. At first mostly a literary public, or community, it rapidly turned into a public whose opinion on matters political and social outran the original quarrel about literature. A special feature of the new public was the participation of women. They not only read the novels but wrote many of them. Their taste, it was argued, was finer than that of the male sex. In the civilizing process, their gentility wooed men from their uncouth pursuit of power by military means. Thus, the central role of the female became a litmus test for deciding what constituted civilization (a new term introduced in 1756, by the elder Mirabeau).[6]

Women were also more sensitive, it was asserted. The notion of *sensibilité* carried with it new rules for human relationships and an awareness of the individual self. Such sensibility marked another advantage of the modern over the ancient. It, too, correlated with an advance in science. William Harvey in 1626 announced his discovery of the circulation of the blood. Now there was a medical basis—new—for understanding the heart, and thus human emotions. These were now placed on a more secure and lofty foundation than could be found in antiquity.

Perrault took advantage of this discovery so as to extend its obvious superiority over the ancients to the domain of both sensibility and moral philosophy. As he wrote, "Just as anatomy has discovered in the heart valves, fibers, and movements of which the ancients had no knowledge, in the same manner moral philosophy [la morale] has discovered attractions, aversions, desires, and repulsions unknown to the ancients."[7] There is a unity of knowledge, so to speak, a holistic joining of the natural and human sciences (as we would come to call them). Such a unity can be expressed in the device of a century and awarded the palm over earlier centuries, that is, those of antiquity. Hence, it is on many separate fronts, but all part of one overall battle that the moderns can be judged the victors qualitatively, even if most of their contemporaries believed otherwise.

(4)

Yet, the picture above is too simple. As with actual war, friends and foes became indistinct, false redoubts had been stormed, and confusion reigned over the battlefield in Tolstoyean fashion. Indeed, it appears now that the wrong terrain had been fought over by some of the partisans of modernity. It is hard, when all is said and done, to sustain the notion that Aeschylus was truly inferior to Corneille, and Homer a lesser bard than members of the French Academy. As is now recognized, literature is the reflection of a society's soul, and thus not subject to the strictures of rational progress. Therefore it was the weakest point on which to base an argument for the superiority of the moderns. Nevertheless it was here that the first flag was planted, and the lines of battle first drawn up. And the first victory of the moderns wrongfully recorded.

A more decisive battleground was that of science. Indeed, within a few years of the *Parallele* and the *Digression*, the war moved across the Channel and took on, almost by accident, another aspect. This time the essential difference between the ancients and the moderns was contested, centrally, in regard to science, per se. Again, the situation could not have been more chaotic and chancy. In 1690, Sir William Temple, a very muddled thinker, published his "An Essay on Ancient and Modern Learning," primarily as a response to Fontenelle. In a farrago of pretended learning, Temple not only took up the cause of ancient literature but also, as one author so well puts it, "defended the science, the learning, the wisdom of antiquity." As he concludes, this "was not easy in the age in which the French were Cartesians, the English Newtonians."[8] What is readily apparent is that Temple was making the same error in regard to science that Perrault had made in regard to literature: fighting on the weakest salient. What was perhaps worse, Temple's ancients were, as it turned out, mostly mystics and frauds of one sort or another.

What followed was a battle of the scholars, with now mostly forgotten names such as William Wotton, Richard Bentley, and Charles Boyle putting their minds in the line of fire, mainly about an obscure writer named Phalaris (probably mythical). In the midst of all this smoke appeared the figure of a novice, Temple's secretary, by the name of Jonathan Swift. In three printed volleys, A Tale of a Tub, The Mechanical Operation of the Spirit, and the Battle of the Books, written mostly in 1697–98, though not published until 1704, he opened a whole new front, satirical in nature. In the Battle of the Books, for example, it is the tomes themselves that fight, with great fun made of the paladins of the modern. If satire could kill, the moderns would have been done in.

About twenty years later, Swift wrote Gulliver's Travels, attacking science and learning rather than literary figures. Swift, unlike his patron, Temple, was not ignorant about science. He attacked it, therefore, as one scholar comments, not as wrong but as "corrupting, dangerous, insane, and ultimately inhuman." This was "a more serious charge than error or pedantry."[9] Swift's great novel is a savage and unforgiving assault on the savagery inherent in science—or at least inherent in the humans who practice it, putting it to work in warfare and human exploitation. And insofar as science is a key element in the modern, Swift's is a powerful onslaught on the entire body and mind of modernity as conceived at the time. And perhaps of any time.

I think it can be fairly said that, as a result of his corrosive writing, Swift won the battle of the books. But the moderns won the war. That is, the proponents of the modern continued their seemingly relentless advance, seizing the ramparts of thought. Material forces were also on their side, and the progress of society was made manifest by technological and scientific developments. Swift had made fun of them, but such fun did not make them disappear.

The battle of the ancients and the moderns was an emblematic struggle. In itself a kind of commedia dell'arte, it did signal a victory of the moderns and all that followed from it. The triumph of the moderns marked a shift from an attempt to gain significant footholds for the forces of modernity to a largely dominant position for its proponents. It left them in command of the intellectual field of the eighteenth century.

(5)

However designated—quarrel, parallel, or battle—the confrontation that started in Western Europe at the beginning of the seventeenth century and crested at its end marked the first real multiple of modernity. Its vicissitudes became the model for the subsequent phases of any reach toward that category by which to see the world and its inhabitants. With this statement as our starting point, I want to step back from the details offered above and indulge in a few generalizations.

At modernity's core was an attack on tradition. This is most clearly seen with Bacon, who believed knowledge could not advance without repudiating or at least challenging the so-called verities of the past.[10] Perrault wrote his *Siecle* and his *Parellele* in the same spirit. For them, tradition meant the hoary Aristotelian beliefs and the unexamined notions of the medieval world. A new world, as discovered, for example, in the late fifteenth century, meant new mental horizons as well. The shibboleths of the past were outmoded in the same way that the maps of cartography had to be newly drawn.

In fact, tradition was itself a new concept, brought into being in contrast with the modern. It was the necessary "other," allowing modernity to construct itself and its own identity. In future battles, whatever the content of the prevailing tradition, it was the foil against which modernity could assert itself. If anything, tradition had to be invented so that the battle could take place. Today, of course, we are aware that most traditions are of recent origin: for example, Scottish kilts only go back a few hundred years. For tradition to be meaningful, however, a kind of historical amnesia has to come into play. The origins of a tradition must be forgotten, and its existence for ever assumed.

All modernities, therefore, conjure up a tradition of their own. Indeed, each tradition is a reflection of the modernity before it, an accumulation of the past and the present against which the new modernity must define itself in battle. The current modern becomes traditional and needs to be attacked. The tradition/modern dialectic is, therefore, a constant feature of modernity. Here we have a generalization that gives us additional understanding of the details of any particular phase of modernity.

A second observation to be made about the seventeenth-century battle of the ancients and the moderns is that it was also about religion. Not made obvious in the writings of Perrault, who concentrated on literature and technology, religion nevertheless provided the overall context in which the struggle took place. One scholar, Jonathan Israel, puts it bluntly: "What was at stake were two opposed visions of the world, one based on Revelation, religion, and miracles, the other rejecting these in favour of a philosophical determinism and materialism rooted in the idea that there is no divine governance of the world and no hereafter." At the time of the classic battle waged by Perrault, this took the specific form of "a deep and abiding split between philosophical conservatives, broadly the scholastic Aristotelians and innovators, primarily Cartesians, intent on revolutionizing not just philosophy but also physics, astronomy, medicine, and in some respects even Bible criticism and theology, along the lines of Descartes's mechanistic world-view."[11]

At one time it was fashionable to think and write of a battle between theology (note that this is not exactly the same as religion) and science. Recent history of science and a general mood of relativism and ecumenicalism has eroded if not ended this simple view of things. Modern scholarship has shown convincingly that many early scientists were religious at the same time that they were scientific. Believing that in the latter guise they were simply pursuing the footsteps of God, men like Hooke and Boyle saw no conflict in their work. However, while this is so as a matter of history, I think it neglects or downplays the principle involved: that Revelation and Scientific Method are opposed ways of reaching knowledge and fundamentally seek a different kind of knowledge. There is, in short, a battle between religion and science at the heart of modernity. Such an assertion, of course, flies in the face of much of our present-day culture.

Deferring further discussion of this vital topic, I want simply to observe that the history of modernity, starting as it does in seventeenth-century Western Europe, is characterized by major battles between religion, generally conjoined to tradition, and science, whether of physics or of biology. I must immediately repeat that this is, of course, a simplification. In many times and places, religious people have led the fight against tradition. Rarely, however, is it in the name of modernity. Sometimes the latter is an unintended consequence. With this said, we are still left with an acceptable generalization that pits the religious way of thinking against the scientific, with both being parties to the dialectic taking distinct shapes at particular times.

The themes of concern with tradition and of the contrasting visions held by religion and science are recurrent ones in all multiples of modernity. So too is the entwinement of the ensuing battles with politics. The coming of modernity is inseparable from the surrounding struggles for power. We need to remember that contemporaneous with Perrault's *Parallèle* was the English Revolution of 1687–88, the Glorious Revolution. What was in England a political overturn was matched across the Channel at the time by a cultural revolution, a rolling around of intellectual power. This can be seen as a forerunner of the events of 1789. In the case of Perrault, as we noted, his cultural revolution was in the name of the king, Louis le Grand. Yet, in the unanticipated ways of history, that cultural change, the establishing of the supremacy of the moderns over the ancients, was the prerequisite for a much broader political and social upheaval to come: the French Revolution.

Quarrel, parallel, or battle—these are the terms in which the coming of modernity was proclaimed. Given its future connection to revolution, the latter term—battle—seems most suitable. It emphasizes the change brought about by conflict between upholders of an old order and proponents of a new. Tradition, theology, and the political nature of society, in which a new actor, the public, has been brought on to the stage—these are major features of the emerging modernity. As modernity continues to develop and reveal its varied forms in the decades after the end of the seventeenth century, we need to keep our eyes on these fundamental features even as their costumes and spoken lines change.

### (7)

Once modernity has arrived, there appears to be no turning back. A three-hundred-year battle has raged, and, indeed, is still going on in one form or another. What one present-day scholar calls European civil war has predominated throughout that time. As Göran Therborn explains, "By civil war I mean conflicts—usually but not necessarily always violent—for and against a particular social or cultural order within a given population, i.e., within a population with certain recognized connectiveness and boundaries."[12] We, for our part, can enlarge this notion of civil war and extend it to the whole world. Modernity from early on has been not just a European battle, but a global one.

In the process, moderns have become conscious of their modernity. This is the prime significance of the watershed year, 1687–8, and its parallels between the ancients and the moderns. It remained for a matching consciousness to arise, that of antimodernity, a gradual awakening in subsequent years after Perrault and his contemporaries. Henceforth the civil war everywhere can be said to be between moderns and antimoderns, rather than between the ancients and the moderns. In one sense, of course, we can see that struggle as occurring between a given modernity and its successor modernity, displacing the earlier form. In another sense, it appears as a more primordial[13] struggle between what, for example, the German sociologist Tönnies labeled *Gemeinschaft und Gesellschaft*, community and society, eternal verities versus ephemeral fashions and novelties.

All over the world the ramifications of the different viewpoints embodied in the phrase *moderns and antimoderns*, whose ways of thinking go back to the seventeenth century in Western Europe, are on display. A relatively contemporary, less sociological, expression of the battle is typically to be found in the founding statements during the twentieth century, for example, of the Muslim Brotherhood. Thus, in 1928, Hassan al-Banna wrote an essay, "Between Yesterday and Today," in which he resumed the now ancient quarrel in Islamic terms. Attacking the colonialist Europeans, he wrote, "They imported their half-naked women into these regions [Egypt], together with their liquors, their theaters, their dance halls, their amusements, their stories, their newspapers, their novels, their whims, their silly games, and their vices. . . . The day must come when the castles of this materialistic civilization will be laid low upon the heads of their inhabitants."[14]

Here we have a potpourri definition of one version of modernity. Modernity's offences for al-Banna are clearly also temptations. His disciple, Sayyid Qutb, who had experienced elements of this modernity in an extended visit to the United States, recoiled in a fervent manner that almost appears a measure of its attraction. The same story could be told of many American fundamentalists, who, exposed to the lures of Babylon—read, for example, New York City—have recoiled in an attempt to save their previous identities. It is, in short, a continuing battle, in many places.

Staying with the Middle East for a moment, a wonderful fictional treatment of the modern/antimodern dilemma can be found in the novel *My Name is Red* by the Turkish author Orhan Pamuk. As one reviewer summarizes the book, it deals with the schism "between Westernization [actually, this should be modernity] and the traditional values of Islam [as if these traditional values were fixed]." "Set in the sixteenth century," we are told, "'Red' presents the schism as the incursion of Renaissance painting—representational, three-dimensional, and with an individualist vision—into the sultan's court. There the flat, stylized, and impersonal grace of the traditional miniaturists is upheld as a matter of religion; and Western perspective is abhorred, since, for instance, it could make a nearby dog bigger than a far-off mosque."[15]

I quote this particular review because it encapsulates so many of the themes with which I have tried to engage. The review reminds us that the Muslim Brotherhood is only the latest in the reactions of some in the Middle East to a conflict over modernity that is earlier played out in the sultan's court at the time of the late Renaissance, an evidence of the modern even before the full-fledged modernity that I have focused on as emerging a century later in Europe. Pamuk's fictional account is even more salient because it singles out perspective as the focal point of the conflict.

While in this chapter I have tried to indicate the nature of modernity—historical to its core—in terms of the late seventeenth-century battle over literature, technology, religion, and science in Western Europe, I want to turn in various of the chapters that follow to more encompassing aspects of any modernity. The first I propose to tackle is what I am calling the seeing revolution, whose results are all-pervasive partly because they have seeped or swept into our conscious and unconscious way of viewing the world. Linear perspective, as experienced in the sultan's court, is one piece of this story. But, as we shall see, it is itself to be understood as part of a larger narrative dealing with how moderns have come to view the world.

## Notes

1. A good account can be found in Matei Calinescu, *Five Faces of Modernity* (Duke University Press, 1987), 4–22.
2. Miriam R. Levin in *Urban Modernity: Cultural Innovation in the Second Industrial Revolution*, ed. Miriam R. Levin et al. (Cambridge, MIT Press, 2010), 8-9.
3. Ulrich Lehmann, *Tigersprung,* Fashion in Modernity (Cambridge, MIT Press, 2000), 144. This is one of the most original but neglected sources on the entire subject of Modernity.
4. See Joan DeJean, *Ancients Against Moderns.* Culture Wars and the Making of a Fin de Siècle (University of Chicago Press, 1997), 49. This is a most valuable book.
5. *Tigersprung,* op. cit., 144.
6. See my book, *Civilization and Its Contents* (Stanford University Press, 2004).
7. Quoted in DeJean; op. cit., 110.
8. Noel M. Swerdlow, "An Essay on Ancients and Moderns, with a Consideration of Jonathan Swift on Science" (unpub. paper given at the Harvard History of Science Center, April 4, 2000) p. 1. This is a most informed article.
9. Ibid, p.10.
10. For more on Francis Bacon, see my book *The Uncertain Sciences* (Yale University Press, 1998), passim and critical bibliography.
11. Jonathan Israel, *Radical Enlightenment. Philosophy and the Making of Modernity 1650-1750* (Oxford University Press, 2002), 80 and 24. This is an enormously erudite book arguing that

the Enlightenment had its true beginnings in Spinoza and the Netherlands in the seventeenth century.

12. Göran Therborn, *European Morality and Beyond*: The Trajectory of European Societies. 1945–2000 (SAGE, 1995), 21.

13. In fact, I and most scholars today are not very sympathetic to the idea of what is called "primordial." Looked at closely, the primordial turns out to be like tradition, a constructed and changing entity.

14. *The New Yorker*, 7/12/04, 76. Many scholars scorn the use of such sources as this magazine. I think this misplaced snobbery, for some of the most informed and insightful articles are to be found in its pages (along with wonderful cartoons).

15. *The New York Times*, 8/10/04, B6.

# 2

# A Seeing Revolution: A View of Modernity

The distinguished poet and essayist Octavio Paz has declared that all contemporary societies are "condemned to modernity."[1] A certain pejorative accent seems to hover over his pronouncement—we condemn criminals—but, in fact, Paz is generally on the side of the modernists. But what is this modernity to which, for better or worse, he sentences us?

I will try to answer the question by analyzing a key aspect of an attitude, a way of looking at the world that we can recognize as modern. This attitude can be conscious or unconscious. No matter. It is such a pervasive and persistent part of our existence—everyone's existence—that it is inescapable. In this sense, I am arguing, we are indeed condemned to be modern.

This is so even in the case of those who have never given a thought to modernity or, if they have, are antimodern. The battles have been and are mainly a matter for intellectuals, and most people will never have heard of them. Yet, certain aspects of modernity are in the air, and as long as one breathes cannot be avoided. They dictate the way in which we both conceive the universe and the way in which, more instrumentally, we live our lives. They shape the way we see the world, and it is therefore fitting that my first exposition will deal with what I am calling the seeing revolution.

Much of what I will deal with in this regard is part of what has come to be called the scientific revolution. It refers to a burst of scientific work and theory in the seventeenth century, in Europe. Though the term scientific revolution was not used until the twentieth century, three centuries earlier the notion of revolution was in the air. Contemporaries sensed it in regard to politics, and vaguely realized that the changes in science were of so dramatic a nature as to demand an expression other than gradualism. No term for this rapid transformation was then available, and the problem was submerged in the broader struggle of the battle of the ancients and the moderns.

As we have seen, one piece of this conflict concerned the struggle between a religious and a more secular and scientific viewpoint. Rising above the historical to and fro, and the mixed and muddled encounters, of such a struggle, I am postulating a difference between the two viewpoints in principle. Both viewpoints can be said to revolve around the deeply held visions that I shall now describe to be found in each.

Science is a way of seeing things that involves envisioning them according to a method—the scientific method—that emphasizes empirical evidence and theories about such evidence, with the theories being tested by further resort to new evidence. And ad infinitum. Dogma has no place in such a conception of the material world. Religion, on the other hand, literally *has* visions, that is, revelations, which are believed on grounds of faith. They cannot be questioned by any appeal to material evidence. One sees the world in the light of these revelations, delivered by particular prophets, and which are vouchsafed to man miraculously. One applies them to this world rather than looking to the world to test their veracity. They are timeless and unchanging.

In tackling the seeing revolution as a prime factor in modernity, I will start with Copernicus, and then work out in various ways, initially staying with the scientific revolution of the seventeenth century, and then going forward in different directions. Most of what I recount will not be new; it is the use to which I am trying to put this material that has novelty. Holding our account together is the emphasis on vision, i.e., the changing way of seeing the world scientifically that runs through what we call modernity. If one sees the world in this particular way, then one is living in a modern world, in this respect, willy-nilly.

## (2)

Copernicus was a sixteenth-century Catholic priest, not a seventeenth-century modern scientific thinker. His context was the Renaissance, still half situated in medieval society. We think of the scientific revolution as occurring in Western Europe, but Copernicus was Polish, and Kepler, who followed upon his work, was a Central European. We must remember, therefore, that Western Europe is a state of mind as much as a geographical area. Though Copernicus launched his revolution from the periphery, and a century before the solidification of science as a way of life and method, he should be seen, nevertheless, as the progenitor of it all.

Why? The answer is that at one blow Copernicus knocked Earth out of its position as the center of the universe. The author of *On the Revolution of the Heavenly Bodies* (1543) revolutionized human perspective on both the world and man. He boldly placed himself, mentally, in God's place, and looked at the world and saw that it was heliocentric. From God's perspective, viewing the universe from on high, the Earth was a planet circling the sun, not vice-versa. At one stroke, Copernicus destroyed man's anthropocentric illusions, foremost the belief in his geocentric centricity in the universe.[2]

Three centuries later, Freud spoke of this achievement as the first great blow to human narcissism. Copernicus did not intend such an effect. He was merely simplifying the Ptolemaic circles mathematically. It was all an hypothesis at first, not a description of reality (though it became this later with Kepler and Galileo). After all, God had given man mathematics as not only a tool but a thing of beauty as well. Copernicus's conception, then, was basically an aesthetically religious one—though unexpectedly, one that was to shake the foundations of religion.

Copernicus himself was not a revolutionary. In the "Revolutions of the Heavenly Bodies" he used the word to mean a return to an original position, a simple revolving around a fixed point. Revolution as a word meaning an overturn, rather than a return, only appears a few centuries later, with the Glorious Revolution of 1688. Then begins the transformation of the term into a linear version of time marked by cataclysmic and nonreversible change. Not so with the loyal son of the Catholic Church in the sixteenth century. What came to be called the Copernican Revolution was not his revolution.

Nor was Copernicus's mindset particularly modern, any more than his specific beliefs. He never doubted teleology, nor questioned the Aristotelian forms and substances that dominated thought in his time. He believed completely in perfect circles, and the circle as the perfect form. He adhered to the notion of a fixed sphere beyond Earth. Not for Copernicus the infinite world that seemed to hover beyond his mathematical circles. That conviction was Giordano Bruno's a few decades later, a conviction for which he was burned at the stake. The author of the "Revolutions" died quietly in his bed.

Yet, unintended as it was by its author, a Copernican revolution of major dimensions did sweep over the Western world. Appearances were shown to be false; henceforth everything was to be questioned, and a deeper reality to be discovered. Mathematics was one way of penetrating to a deeper reality; other ways might also claim validity.

The new creator of the world—Copernican man—found himself, in the Polish astronomer's conception, still on a stable platform and in a fixed abode, on Earth. Earth, however, was no longer a center of the universe. If this were so, then what matter that Jerusalem was considered by some to be the center of Earth? The tremors of human dislocation could already be detected by sensitive ears.

Copernicus himself would have recoiled in horror at the consequences contained in his writing, but the work was to take on a meaning beyond his restricted imaginings. After Copernicus, the world—the human abode—was a different place in a different space. His work had sent Earth metaphorically, if not literally, spinning out into the new world of modernity. The importance of this shift cannot be exaggerated. Our calendars, perhaps, should be reworked in terms of BC and AC—before and after Copernicus—to reflect this epochal transformation.

## (3)

As Newton famously remarked, he was able to see farther because he stood on the shoulders of giants. Copernicus was one; others I want to touch on briefly for our purposes are Kepler and Galileo. Their names symbolize the way in which an important strand of modernity consists of the accumulation and expansion of scientific knowledge. Though my focus here is on the seeing aspect of that revolutionary growth, it is well also to note the general observation.

Kepler, of course, is best known for giving mathematical extension and expression to Copernicus's understanding of heliocentricity. His famous laws concerning the elliptical path of the planets are still a fixture of the firmament as we know it. Less well known to the average person is his work in optics. Yet for our purposes it is one of the parts that is most important. As Svetlana Alpers tells us, Kepler turned his attention from the firmament to the instrument with which we view it. From what is looked at to how we look at it.[3] (Coincidentally, one can see prefigured here the shift in seventeenth- to eighteenth-century philosophy from ontology to epistemology.)

In a 1604 publication, *Astronomia pars Optica* (The Optical Part of Astronomy), the eye itself became the object of Kepler's inquiry. He treated it as a mechanical device, an optical lens for focusing on objects. He analyzed its properties, including its propensity to distortion and error. Rather than a reflection of the human soul, the eye is simply a lens through which we can look at nature near and far. Thus, the eye has been objectified. What we see, say, as a planet, is dictated by how we see it. However, any implicit relativism is obviated by the application of mathematics, which gives us eternal and fixed laws. Yet, as can readily be seen, Kepler's work in optics, as with Copernicus's heliocentric theory, carried revolutionary implications, of which relativism was one.

When Kepler, who was already a Copernican as a result of his own earlier work in mathematics, learned in 1610 of Galileo's discoveries with what was then called a spyglass (Galileo's own term was *perspicillum*), he immediately set about acquiring and using one. By the next year he had published his *Dioptrice*, where he explored the theory behind the instrument. Thus he made another advance in establishing the modern theory of optics.

By means of this new science Kepler was able to lead his contemporaries toward a more modern way of seeing the world. It was a mathematical and objective manner of viewing

things. He had moved from earlier training in theology—
Kepler was a Lutheran, who suffered for his affiliation during the Thirty Years War—to an appointment as a professor
teaching arithmetic and geometry at the Protestant seminary
in Graz (Austria). His work in astronomy was counterbalanced
by his work in astrology. He also worked on chronology,
publishing in 1614 his *Concerning the True Year in which the
Son of God Assumed a Human Nature in the Uterus of the Blessed
Virgin Mary*: it was 4 BC, after the errors in the then reigning
Christian calendar were corrected. Thus, in his own life and
work we can see how he negotiated between the two visions
of religion and science.

For him, however, there was not the clear separation that
we see now. Rather, he seems to have viewed the two as on
a spectrum. This is the historical actuality. The principal
result, however, was a gradual supplanting of the religious
perspective by the scientific one. Concretely expressed in his
three laws of planetary motion, in his actual work in optics,
and in his employment of the telescopic instrument whose
principles he had investigated to observe Jupiter's satellites,
Kepler's scientific achievements ended by helping to displace
the religious viewpoint. If one can so put it, the dross of earlier
tradition dropped off in the process of scientific accumulation to which I referred earlier.

(4)

The next shoulder on which scientific modernity stood was
Galileo. Indeed, he and Kepler were contemporaries, who
supported one another's work. Galileo, too, moved steadily
from the world of religion to that of secular science. As a
youth he seriously considered joining a religious order, that
of the Camadolese monks, whose monastery had split many
centuries earlier from the Benedictine Order. Instead, however, pushed by his father, Galileo turned halfheartedly to

the study of medicine. Only gradually did he find his way to mathematics, and a career as an astronomer. In this latter role we still find a thread linking him to his earlier career forays when early on he lectured to medical students at Padua in Florence who needed some knowledge of astrology in their practice. Even more to this point was his previous invited lecture to the Academy in Florence on the dimensions and location of hell in Dante's *Inferno*!

As a mathematical astronomer, Galileo supported his friend Kepler's arguments for the appearance of a new star in 1604 (a supernova). This was a direct challenge to the Aristotelian belief that the realm of the fixed stars was permanent. It was Galileo's learning about the new spyglass in 1609 constructed by a "certain Fleming," however, that marked the real beginning of his revolutionary turn to support of the Copernican system. Within a year, Galileo had improved the instrument and used it to observe the bodies of outer space. In 1610 he published the *Starry Messenger*, with its claims to having seen mountains on the moon and small orbiting bodies around Jupiter. These he called the "Medicean stars" in order to curry favor with his patron, Cosimo de Medici.

Prospering in his career, Galileo continued to observe the heavens, spotting sunspots, and going further in his work on dynamics and the mechanics of falling bodies. In this work he could employ experiments, for example, by using a pendulum to measure the speed of falling bodies. The most famous experiment, of course, was the supposed dropping of weights from the tower of Pisa in order to show that objects did not fall behind the tower on a rotating Earth, as predicted by the opponents of his theory. In fact, the experiment seems to have been a thought experiment, but no less an experiment for all that.

As long as Copernicus and his followers claimed that heliocentricity was only a mathematical calculation and not a reality, they could escape the charge of heresy. Both Kepler and Galileo, however, boldly went beyond Copernicus in this regard, and defended heliocentricity as an actual part of nature. Their work henceforth was to explain how this mechanism worked. The implications for traditional belief and how the world would henceforth be viewed were consequently shattering. The culmination for Galileo was his trial in 1632, his censure by the Church authorities, and his house arrest for the rest of his days (few).

On the way to his trial, so to speak, Galileo had made clear that the heliocentric theory was not only mathematical, but a description of reality. Further, he not only indicated the schism between the Copernican theory and holy scriptures but challenged the latter on its own terrain. Extending his suspicion of books in general, for he preferred going straight to nature itself, he questioned the Bible as being open to misreading. First he declared that God is no less "excellently revealed in Nature's actions than in the sacred statements of the Bible." Then he questioned the extension of religious authorities into the physical sciences, where they demanded that, as Galileo put it, we should "altogether abandon reason and the evidence of our senses in favor of some biblical passage."[4]

Advancing his modern views in such works as a *Letter to the Grand Duchess* (1616), and then his classic *Dialogue Concerning the Two Chief Systems of the World–Ptolemaic and Copernican* (begun in 1624 and published in 1632), Galileo was increasingly treading on dangerous ground. It was the latter work, however, that finally led to the judicial proceedings against him. Galileo used the term *Dialogue*; we in our turn can refer to it as a new version of the parallel, quarrel, or battle of the ancients and moderns that we discussed earlier. In the fullest sense, then, his trial was a continuation of the struggle over the coming of modernity.

We have been soaring high above Galileo's actual work—his contributions in regard to pendulums, inclined planes, planetary motion, and so on, all of which would figure in a standard history of science account—to concentrate on some of the implications of his work for our subject. The natural science itself, of course, entered into the accumulated nature of modern science, becoming a possession of all humanity. By itself, this development would make Galileo a modern hero.

I want to single out, however, a few more powerful implications of the great Italian's work in science. The first is that Galileo took another giant step beyond anthropomorphism, or the human propensity to see nature in its own image. Instead, Galileo insisted upon self-effacement, the removal of the human ego from its effort to observe and understand physical nature. Where in astrology, for example, the heavens are anthropomorphized, in astronomy the heavens were to be studied objectively. Obliquely he had said this earlier when trying to detach astronomy from the all-too-human scriptures, quoting an eminent ecclesiastic to the effect that "the intention of the Holy Ghost is to teach us how one goes to heaven, not how heaven goes." This sentiment was echoed in his reputed sotto voce comment after having been forced to repudiate the Copernican doctrine at his trial: "But still they [the stars] move."

Paradoxically, removing religion from scientific observation, Galileo went further along the line trod by his friend Kepler. As we have seen, Copernicus had imaginatively placed himself in God's mind. It is only a short step from this way of seeing things to viewing man himself as godlike. The Christian religion, of course, embraced this notion—Christ is both God and man—but what modern science in the form of Galileo and his confreres had done was to secularize the notion. To continue tracing this idea would carry us to Descartes, who arrogantly claimed that his mathematical construction of the universe would have to be followed by God himself; that is, he would be constrained to create the universe just as the Frenchman had created it.

The second major implication I wish to focus on concerns appearances and reality. With Galileo, the telescope is used to see beyond appearances (we shall see later that the same is true in the case of microscopes). Appearances can be deceptive. In a Platonic vein, Galileo indicates a reality, such as moons revolving around Jupiter. Unlike Plato, however, the Italian is not talking about an ideal form reached by the mind, but an empirical reality grasped by the use of instruments and experiments. While mathematics is certainly Platonic in one sense, its use by the scientific revolutionaries of the seventeenth century is applied so as to go beyond appearances.

The scientific approach is to go directly to nature, by our own observations, using a combination of instruments and mathematics. The scientist sees for himself, and not through the eyes of some traditional authority. Books are a secondary source, and to be used critically and as a last resort. This includes the Bible, as we have seen in the case of Galileo. What is said there must be placed before the bar of reason, a reason supported by the scientific method. While revelation is given lip service, the voice of science speaks in firm tones. Secularism trumps sectarianism.

(5)

With Copernicus, Kepler, and Galileo I have tried to sketch the way in which the first stages of the seeing revolution occurred. The widespread acceptance of linear perspective in Europe is a development marked less by the presence of great names. It is also one in which art and architecture rather than astronomy are at the center. The end result is similar: we see the world in a different shape from that of the ancients and inhabitants of the middle ages. While this manner of seeing will itself be overturned and replaced in the twentieth century, with its nonrepresentational painting, it prevailed for over four centuries earlier and still persists in important ways.

We can bear witness to this perspectival revolution by looking, for example, at a painting by Giotto. In this thirteenth-century painting, it matters not whether a figure is in the foreground or background; its size will not depend on the space it occupies but on its spiritual importance. Thus, the shape of Jesus even if far in the background will loom larger than mundane objects toward the front of the picture. By the time of Leonardo and his fellow painters of the sixteenth century, all this has changed. Now it is geometry, not theology, that determines what is large and what is small in the painting. It is the method of linear perspective that gives shape to the world and human representation of it. Here, too, even in religious paintings, the secular eye is brought to bear.

It is true that we find hints of this new method in antiquity, for example in the scenic paintings that serve as backdrop for the plays of Aeschylus, Sophocles, and Euripides. The possibility of linear perspective is then given a sure footing in Euclid's geometry, and in the time of the Romans by Ptolemy's *Geographia*. In this brief sketch of the subject we must next jump to the fourteenth century in Italy, with the reappearance of Ptolemy's work, and its further development by Brunelleschi, who, using a mirror, demonstrated linear perspective in the course of his experiments. It remained only for Alberti to carry the new method into painting, writing a treatise showing how to draw in the new way.

The end result was a further revolution in seeing. Visual space was now a matter of an abstract, uniform system of linear coordinates, ordered in an a priori and fixed manner. One single vantage point gave entry into the painter's world. That point was necessarily the same for every viewer. The world is objectivized and mathematicized. As one scholar sums it up, linear perspective "demanded that all space, celestial and terrestrial alike, be perceived as having the same physical properties and obeying the same geometrical rules."[5]

The results are far-reaching. On one side, it starts from inside the human observer, a subject, who is now in a position to distance himself from what he sees and to make it into a matter of scientific observation. Humanistic and subjective at the beginning, such subjectivism nevertheless becomes objective because everyone must see from the same viewpoint. On the other side, the same optical principles reach out to the mappings of the cartographer Toscanelli—with his probable influence on Columbus—and of Ortelius and Mercator. We have set sail with the modern-day Ulysses, guided by linear perspective, to a new world, beyond the setting sun.

We do not find such a view, for example, in fifteenth-century China. Unknown to it was linear perspective and all the modern consequences that flow from that way of seeing. China still viewed its world largely in traditional ways. In the West, however, a change in seeing had occurred, as manifested in the shift from Giotto to Leonardo. For some scholars, the lack of linear perspective was a key element in China itself not bringing about or participating in the early-seventeenth-century scientific revolution.

An additional consequence was that not only the natural world was seen in objective terms but the social world as well. Both Chinese and European societies in the twelfth and fifteenth centuries were hierarchical; but the new perspective was shaking not only the pillars of Hercules, the promontories around Gibraltar, by going beyond them, but the pillars of existing Western society. One began to look at it differently. The geometrical nature of linear perspective implied that all parts of space were equal. Into such a space, eventually, could step more or less equal players in the drama of social existence. Of course, this outcome was merely potential, and many other factors would necessarily be involved. Its realization in the West would take at least another couple of centuries. Not inevitable, the shift in social space was none-theless correlative with the revolution that had taken place in mathematized space, and made manifest in the canvases of Leonardo and his fellow Renaissance painters.

There was another space besides the mathematical and social that was being perceived differently in the fifteenth century. Ptolemy's *Geographia*, which played a role in the rise of linear perspective, also led out to a new geography, wherein a continent previously almost completely unknown swam into sight. Partly inspired by the maps of Toscanelli and his fellow geographers, as is well known, Columbus "in 1492, sailed the ocean blue" and discovered America. However mixed his notions—he thought that he was finding a direct route to India—however medieval some of his inspirations—he was carrying out the Christian mission—however materialist his aims—he was conquering new territories for Castile and gold and silver for his royal patron and himself—he altered irreme-diably the consciousness of humanity. He hinted that we live on a globe, a fact made more evident by Magellan's naviga-tion around the world. The subsequent ubiquity of globes, sitting on the desks of scholars and rulers depicted in so many Renaissance paintings, attest to Columbus's achievement.

The consequences of seeing a new world—discovering it—are both immediate and long range, identifiable and incalculable. Humanity has not only uncovered a New World, geographically, but entered one, spiritually. Henceforth everything will carry the stamp of a possible newness, which is a major characteristic of the modern. We can explore this newness by singling out three of its major features.

The fifteenth-century explorations—and we must remember that they actually start before Columbus, with efforts to sail around the coast of Africa—opened up a new world of flora and fauna, entailing a startling explosion of knowledge in the emerging field of natural history. Plants and animals hitherto unknown in Europe now are brought home to be put in the herbariums, zoos, and *wonder* cabinets that have suddenly become fashionable. Comparative zoology and comparative botany, even though nameless as such at the time, spring into life. Though the term biology must wait until the turn of the eighteenth century to be coined, nature can now potentially be seen in new terms. Not only as objective—existing outside of man—but as taking on a life of its own that, a few centuries later, will break apart the great chain of being.[6]

Next among the fauna coming from the new world was a new man. The misnamed Indians, of both North and South America, posed a puzzling problem. Were they to be viewed as truly human, with souls to be saved? Or cannibals, beyond the human pale, fit only to be banished from existence, or enslaved? In short, what did it mean to be human? Further, they lived in societies very different from those of the Europeans. Which was the more natural? Or were all societies just different? In sum, a new mirror was being held up to European man, not just in his home and in the studio of painters, but in the wilds of America.

Such questions were not entirely new. Europeans knew of other peoples—the Chinese, the Turks—who were different from them, and of other times, Greek and Roman. In fact, the case can be made that the Turkish threat was the main stimulant in early modern Europe's effort to define its own identity at the time. Such encounters, however, had always been with what were, in fact, viewed as superior or similar levels of civilization (to use that anachronistic term, for the reified noun, as mentioned earlier, was not coined until 1756).

Thus, the third major novelty was that the encounter with the natives or savages of the New World moved the dialogue to a whole new level. It is the beginning of the awareness of the true other, of someone so radically different from oneself, or so it seems, as to make one's self newly problematic. The subjective in this encounter with objectivity, meaning human phenomena that are to be viewed as outside oneself—subject to scientific observation and from an external perspective—takes on a new nature.

(6)

I want to conclude our foray into the seeing revolution by a more sustained look at some of the instruments that helped bring about the change. The change involved a way of seeing that we have come to call *modern*. Moderns simply came to see a different world, and to see it differently than their predecessors. This optical transformation was spurred forward by a number of inventions. Eyeglasses can be considered the first such innovation, probably originating in China, and then being refined into spectacles in the fourteenth century. They did not so much change the way we view the world, however, as maintain our ability to see it, combating myopia, for example. What they did do, in addition, was to concentrate attention on how images might be mechanically altered.

The telescope, which we have already noted, and the microscope were more critical to the seeing revolution. Both magnified the world—one the macrocosm, the other the microcosm, the far and the near, the large and the small. These two new glasses are twin forces, unknown to antiquity. They combine to push the mind and the mind's eye toward a common vision at the same time that, separately, they open different vistas as to our conception of nature.

To be sure, the telescope was applied to an ancient science, astronomy. However it was only in the seventeenth century that the improved telescope, as developed in conjunction with work on the microscope, truly opened up the heavens in detail to the human eye. When Galileo, for example, trained his telescope on Jupiter and saw its moons he saw what no other human before him had perceived. How could he and his contemporaries not feel superior to the ancients?

The microscope, in contrast, was utterly unknown to the ancients. Its development by the Dutch pioneers Anthony van Leeuwenhoek and Jan Swammerdam turned the human gaze downward, to an unknown world lurking below ordinary appearances. Into the new glass swam hitherto unperceived monsters and monstrously enlarged features, such as the eye of a fly.

Contemporaries were overwhelmed by the dual new worlds into which their optical instruments had drawn them. Groping for suitable metaphors, they kept comparing the previously unknown worlds of the far and the near to the New World discoveries of a few centuries earlier. Typical was Robert Hooke's rotund encomium, where he confessed his hope to be able to "promote the use of mechanical helps for the Senses, both in the surveying of the already visible world, and for the discovery of many hitherto unknown, and to make us with the great Conqueror, to be affected that we have not yet overcome one World when there are so many others to be discovered, every considerable improvement of Telescopes or Microscopes producing new Worlds and Terra-Incognita's to our view."[7] Another observer, training a telescope on the moon, exclaimed, "my diligent Galileus hath done more in his three fold discoveries than Magellane in opening the streightes to the South sea or the dutch men that were eaten by beares in Nova Zembla."[8]

It all went together: the excitement of glimpsing new shores and inhabitants of the globe, and the exaltation of peering through the telescope and microscope and discovering new bodies in the heavens and novel forms of life in the miniature seas swimming beneath one's lens. Hooke's prose itself seemed in its own excessive and disordered state to resemble the expanding, unmapped worlds opened up by the seeing revolution. Constantijn Huygens was more succinct in his poetic rendition of the impact of the new instruments:

> At last mortals may, so to speak, be like gods,
> If they can see far and near, here and everywhere.[9]

Ornately or simply expressed, contemporaries were thunder-struck by the revelations disclosed to them by the telescope and the microscope. Their senses had been overwhelmed and vastly extended by the new mechanical devices.

Such was the combined effect of the telescope and the microscope. As remarked earlier, they also had differential effects. The telescope was employed in astronomy, and combined with mathematics to construct a mechanical universe. Its reach by the end of the century was to eventuate in a Newtonian "system of the world," where the system was modeled on the supreme technological achievement of the time, the clock. This world was characterized by simplicity, and by reduction to the fewest laws and phenomena.

The microscope carried men's eyes in another direction. It focused mostly on living matter and as Edward G. Ruestow has put it, "testified to an evermore intricate complexity in nature and a pervasive and continuing unexpectedness."[10] In short, the scientific revolution of the period was pulled by "two contrasting aesthetics" and in two directions: the mechanical and the vital. This fact is often obscured by tendentious accounts of seventeenth-century science, and thus its modernity, that often seek to squeeze it simply into a mechanical mold.

Another thing to note is the impact that the two optical inventions had on the contemporary reliance on and praise of sense impressions that we highlighted earlier. Now, these impressions seemed to be called into question. We can no longer believe our senses: such seemed to be the message of the telescope and microscope as they peered beyond or beneath appearances. Hence arose a widespread feeling of disorientation and disordered existence. A pervasive anxiety can be found in many writings of the time, such as in Swift's account of Gulliver's travels in worlds that were both enlarged and diminished.

Paradoxically, at the same time, the appeal to sense impressions as the basis of scientific knowledge was sounded ever more forcefully. Our senses, it was claimed by proponents of this view, were simply enlarged and extended, not undermined. Later, Freud would label man as a "prosthetic God"; as such he was to be eulogized, not deplored. With our increased sensory apparatus, it was argued, we could penetrate further into reality, for reality was what we could see beyond mere surface appearances only with our new eyes.

Here, then, we see a fundamental feature of the new modernity. It was constantly in dialectic with itself, a dialectic that was special because it was carried out in terms of the new sciences and scientific method. It was the very paradoxes of science that kept pushing its practitioners forward into new terrain, freshly perceived. Thus, the prevailing modernity carried within itself its own future remodeling. That was one of the novel features about itself that the modern self of the seventeenth century came to recognize and to accept: about itself and the world. This revolution in consciousness, having started, earlier and hesitantly, with Copernicus, carried with it a ceaseless dynamism, the invention of inventions, so to speak, as a continuous process. Thus was created a modern world, forever restless and moving ahead to yet new modernities.

(7)

The seeing revolution whose outlines I have tried to describe in this chapter obviously had consequences to be found in many directions. A quick summary would focus on a few of the following. Above mundane life, a battle of sorts between the religious and the scientific way of seeing was clearly taking place. Filled with skirmishes, with friendly concords, and with crossovers, the dialogue or debate nevertheless must be viewed as a prominent feature of modernity. Science was gradually displacing religion as a way of seeing. Or to put it better: the religious vision persisted but was gradually rivaled or displaced as the center of human activity by the scientific.

Priya Natrajan has also suggested that the new ways of seeing the world also promoted the rise of individualism.[11] The new knowledge was widely disseminated due to the invention of the printing press. Increasingly removed from the control of the Church, knowledge was being democratized at the same time as it was being secularized.

In the midst of mundane existence, the scientific way of seeing increasingly characterized the modern world. The telescope and its findings influenced navigation and thus trade and exploration. The microscope began to find a place in medicine, joining with anatomy in looking at man as a part of nature, to be seen in naturalistic terms. Linear perspective invaded painting and architecture. The ordinary person did not need to decide to be modern; more and more he was simply living in a modern world. Of course, on the conscious level he or she might decide to be violently antimodern, to envelope the self in traditional, religious vistas; nevertheless, I am arguing, from the seventeenth century on the average person was condemned to be modern in the sense of living in a world whose sight lines he could not avoid seeing, willy-nilly.

Another major consequence of this change in optics was the rise of objectivity and the decline of anthropomorphism. Though the effort to be objective was located in Man himself, this inherent subjectivity was hedged about by tools such as the telescope, microscope, clock, and linear perspective, whose readings were supposed to be the same for all men. Mathematics worked to the same effect. With all such aids, humans presumably could go beyond appearances to a settled and fixed reality, confirmed by everyman's eyes. This was part of what was involved in the battle over the heliocentric theory. The unaided eyes seemed to show the sun rotating around Earth. The aided eye presented us with a corrected vision that was real and not just a matter of mathematical speculation.

Finally, another consequence was that this very way of seeing itself demanded continuing rectification. The lenses by which we view the world need constantly to be reground. Science is always in dialectic with itself. Such re-examination is a fundamental part of the modern. Needless to say, it enters into the human conception of itself, which changes along with the outer world—an outer world that is now seen in endless scientific permutations and new shapes. That transformation of the self, too, is a fundamental part of the modern.

## Notes

1. Quoted in John Tomlinson, *Cultural Imperialism* (London: Continuum, 1991), 140.

2. One of the most important books on the Copernican revolution is Hans Blumenberg, *The Genesis of the Copernican Revolution* (MIT Press, 1987). In general, Blumenberg is one of the most thoughtful and original scholars of our time, whose work has not received the attention it deserves.

3. See Svetlana Alpers, *The Art of Describing* (University of Chicago Press, 1983).

4. Quoted with further discussion by Bruce Mazlish, *The Uncertain Sciences* (1980), 100.

5. See Samuel Y. Edgerton, *The Renaissance Rediscovery of Linear Perspective* (Basic Books, 1975) 17, and other of his books.

6. See Arthur Lovejoy's classic treatment in *The Great Chain of Being* (Harvard University Press, 1936).

7.    Robert Hooke, *Micrographia* (1665), Preface.
8.    Sir William Lower in a letter to Thomas Harriot. Quoted from S. P. Rigaud, *Supplement to Dr. Bradley's Miscellaneous Works: With an account of Harriot's Astronomical Papers* (1833), 25.
9.    Quoted in Svetlana Alpers, op. cit., 17.
10.   Edward G. Ruestow, *The Microscope in the Dutch Republic. The Shaping of Discovery* (Cambridge University Press, 1996), 4.
11.   In private exchanges. I want to acknowledge here my appreciation of her comments.

# 3

# The Self

The seeing revolution was accompanied by a changed notion of what it meant to be a self—in other words, a self that inhabits a scientific world. It is not clear in which direction the causal arrow points; a way of seeing and a way of being reinforce each other. The best word for the relation is correlation (although the great German sociologist Max Weber might speak of affinities). Such a self is modern, and as such a constantly changing and dynamic entity. Self replaces or displaces the older, traditional notion of the soul, and detaches it from its religious ties. In the process self attaches itself to a concept of the individual, which culminates in the idea of individualism.

This process of the developing self does not wait upon the work of scientists such as Kepler and Galileo, but takes its start earlier, in the period of the Renaissance (which means closer to Copernicus). In this sense, the ground is made fertile for the growth of what I am calling a scientific self, yet this earlier sense of the self differs from that latter in important ways. What binds the two—the Renaissance self, described by one scholar as "self-fashioning," and the scientific self— however, is that both throw off the description of the self imposed on it by authorities and collective judgments, and emphasize the self's autonomy. I, an individual, make myself, though in a setting given to me by history and my circumstances (to paraphrase Karl Marx).

According to the great Swiss historian Jacob Burckhardt, it was sometime in the fifteenth century that man first consciously saw himself as an individual. In the Middle Ages, Burckhardt argued, "Man was conscious of himself only as a member of a race, people, party, family, or corporation—only through some general category. In Italy this veil first melted into air [and again we hear the echo of the Swiss author's near contemporary, Marx]; an *objective* treatment and consideration of the State and of all the things of this world became possible."[1] We can pause for a moment to note that objective is the same word that we have seen stressed by scientists in our previous chapter, as a way of seeing the world.

But then Burckhardt continues in a different vein. "The *subjective* side at the same time asserted itself with corresponding emphasis; man became a spiritual *individual*, and recognized himself as such." Thus, on this account, the new self and its individuality is a counterpart to the objective attitude, its other side, so to speak.

The entire passage bears further examination. It occurs in Burckhardt's book *The Civilization of the Renaissance in Italy*. Although the term civilization only arises in the eighteenth century, by employing it anachronistically our historian intends by its usage to impose a unity on the Renaissance in Italy. The "development of the individual" self fits in with the "state as a work of art," the "revival of antiquity," the "discovery of the world and of man," the "society and festivals," and the "morality and religion," all to be found in Italy of the time, and all subtitles in his book.

The individual self is, then, necessarily in a particular social and historical context that fosters the process by which, as another scholar puts it, "modern man matured towards a consciousness of himself."[2] It is because Italy has liberated itself from the constraints of feudalism that the individual can shake himself free from communal identities, at least to a certain extent. Thus, for example, in the realm of painting or sculpture the artist can sign his own name to his work rather than disappearing into the anonymity of the medieval artisan decorating the great Gothic cathedrals. In regard to the state, again, it can be a personal achievement, a work of art as Burckhardt designates it, not a matter of traditional inheritance of Church-sanctified holding. The prince will create the state in his own self-image. The artist will paint self-portraits. Those who can afford mirrors will look into them to see their selves.

We are at the beginning of a long, slow development of what is to become a leading trait in the definition of the modern. In this development, individuality is tied to notions of self and of developing self-consciousness. Each of these terms—self, individuality, and consciousness—will have its own changing and expanding meaning, and yet be connected to its companions. The content of each term may change, and yet the term remains the same. The trait, however, may be held differentially by different classes in the society and subsequently respond to shifts in political and social power. In short, we must focus on a process, which does not unfold in straightforward, deterministic fashion, but moves forward and backward, to one side and then another, yet maintains a momentum that we only recognize from our present vantage point.

## (2)

The romantic portrait of the Renaissance by Burckhardt, with its claim that we find in this period the origins of the modern self, can be subject to criticism. Yet he clearly intuited some of the change that was taking place. It is important, however, to recognize that his self is the humanistic one, to be found in earlier times and different climes, though with variations. It persists as the self becomes a scientific one, but is not the same as the latter. It is the seeing revolution of the seventeenth century that shapes the new sense of the self and therefore introduces us to the modern individual.

We have already taken note of Francis Bacon in our first chapter. As the progenitor of what we have come to call scientific empiricism, he set forth an ideal of science as a cumulative enterprise, going well beyond the authority of the ancients. In this context, he also saw natural science and human science as connected and seamless. As he remarked, "We now come to the knowledge of ourselves . . . since the knowledge of himself is to man the end and time of the sciences, of which nature only forms a part."[3] In Bacon's view, the self can take itself as the object of scientific knowledge and then, avoiding anthropomorphism by embracing the scientific method, project that self outward into nature. In fact, typical of his age, Bacon was a great projector in many ways, one of which was to promote as a project the idea of a new kind of scientific self.

Alongside of Bacon, we also spoke of René Descartes in that initial chapter. Like Bacon, Descartes put forth a new sense of self. It had different qualities than Bacon's, however. The result was that the modernity of the seventeenth century and after was to carry with it, so to speak, a split personality, a divided soul of sorts. In place of the communal scientific self advocated by the English statesman, our French philosopher insisted upon a solitary self, from which the world could then be constructed.

It is revealing that Descartes put forward his views in an autobiographical mode. His *Discourse on Method* tells the story of his life. It has us follow his experiences and his thoughts as they developed in the course of his travels. We see the world through his eyes. Indeed, the autobiography is a particular Western and modern genre (the one early example appears to be Saint Augustine's *Confessions*). In its origins, such a literary portrait is frequently religious, especially Protestant. Descartes's genius was to turn devotional introspection into something like the scientific examination of the soul. The result was a striking affirmation, though unintended by its author, of secular individualism, a major component of the century's modernity, and of variants of later modernities as well.

In a famous phrase, Descartes declared that "I think, therefore I am." Here he combined an emphasis on the ego—the "I"—and his equally famous embrace of reason. The self defines itself as a thinking being. It is, in the Frenchman's account, a being in a vacuum, self-enclosed, removed from any specific culture. It knows itself through its own reasoning powers, and on this unmoved foundation constructs the rest of the world. It is a kind of paradox that this individual reason ends up not really being individual at all, for it is accessible to everyone in the same way. All one need do is follow Descartes's method—his famous rules—to arrive at correct conclusions.

We start with total doubt, the notorious Cartesian skepticism. In complete opposition to Bacon's method, the French thinker announced a profound distrust of our sense impressions: his approach will make "available to us an easy method of accustoming our minds to become independent of the senses." And here we encounter another paradox. Starting with total doubt, except for our ability to think independently of our surrounding world, we reach total certainty. Such certainty is delivered by science, as previously it had been by religion, but by the new method.

Descartes did not merely distrust the senses. He doubted all received knowledge, whether derived from the ancient texts or from local custom. In this he is at one with his English counterpart. Then, although he has also told us to doubt reality—our sense impressions—he lets it in again through the back door, advising us to turn to things as they are, mediated through the mind's reason. The prime form of this reason is mathematical. Thus, Descartes joins hands with his contemporary Galileo and perceives the universe as written in mathematical symbols. It is in this way that we see reality.

The fact is that Descartes implicitly undermined God's power and took it over for himself and his fellow human beings. It is there in his assumption that his reason could reconstruct the world physically, exactly as God had constructed it; in fact, God was constrained by his own laws of creation. It is also present in Descartes's discussion of automata. It was not only machines, such as hydraulic devices, that operated according to mechanical and mathematical principles. It was also animals. Devoid of reason, according to the author of the *Discourse on Method*, animals were moved by reflex action.

Was man any different? Yes, declared Descartes in orthodox tones. Man had a soul, defined as invisible and immaterial. In all other respects, he could be thought of as a machine; having done numerous dissections, Descartes concluded that man was, physiologically, a system of levers and pulleys. Unintentionally, therefore, the way was now open to seeing the soul as a superfluous assumption, with no grounding in reality. If one ignored the fact that man was, in principle, an automaton, the medieval soul could be replaced by the idea of the self, as an autonomous creation, shaping the world around it in scientific fashion. Like science itself the self was a constantly changing, adaptive mechanism. Self and science, each emerged from and supported the other. Such was the modern vision.

Some of the key words in this modernity would be as follows: in regard to nature a distrust of sense impressions, such as the centrality of Earth; a fixation on man as the center of his own world; a reconstruction of that world by man's reason; and an appeal to sense impressions as the ultimate corrective to mere words and misguided reason in the realm of the social as well as the natural. Obviously, some parts of this definition were in opposition to other portions. In short, there was a continuing tension between reason and empirical research that stands at the heart of the new science.

Such is one cluster. Another concerns the self: anthropomorphism—the projection onto nature of man's desires—is distrusted; in its place stands self-creativity, which includes the creation of the outside world; this sense is a skeptical one, doubting everything, while yearning for certainty; such a self is now also a scientific self, constantly questioning itself and all around it in terms of a special method; and it is, finally, a shaken self, bequeathing to modern society a disturbing sense of insecurity.

## (3)

With the Cartesians, the self is a scientific self, having no history and existing as an island unto itself—in regard to the latter, Robinson Crusoe is the prototypic figure. Dominating the seventeenth century as an idea, it persists into the next century, but here it encounters powerful rivals. To treat of them requires us to go beyond the classical modernity of Bacon and Descartes's century—having noted that Bacon offers a variant on the initial scientific self—and study how the notion of the self changes in a historical and developmental direction. It is this self, rather more than the Cartesian, that is in accord with modernity's ceaselessly changing nature.

To understand what happened I will focus on two seminal thinkers: Adam Smith and Georg Friedrich Hegel. Smith's contribution took two forms, incorporated in the two great books that he wrote. The first was the *Theory of the Moral*

*Sentiments* (1759). Here, inquiring into the origins of morality, he advanced his view that self necessarily envisions itself in a social setting. In viewing and reviewing its actions, it appeals not only to its own judgment but to that of what Smith called an "impartial spectator." "What would another person think of my action?" is the question we ask ourselves in regard to what we have done. In the previous chapter, I spoke of a seeing revolution. We encounter another piece of that revolution in Smith's query: how would another person view our actions? In attempting to stand outside ourselves, we seek to approach a subjective form of objectivity.

For many scholars, a break seems to exist between this view of the self as a moral being and that advanced by Smith in his *Wealth of Nations* (1776). I disagree. Smith assumes that the self, newly viewed as it is in the *Theory*, will persist in society as a whole. It is the basis of benevolence. But, he asks, what if we wish to comprehend the realm of exchange, rather than merely of benevolence, in society? What sort of self do we have to postulate for such a situation? For if the modern self is to free itself from the bonds of feudal dependence and the constraints of mercantilism—which it has to do to be modern—it must create an economy of expansion. This it can do by embracing the division of labor and (ideally) a free world market. And in order to do this it needs an expanding and expansive self as actor.

The key to how this takes place is, of course, Smith's famous appeal to self-interest. Not the benevolence of the butcher, baker, and candlestick maker, though this may exist outside the exchange relation, but their sense of self-gain will be activated in economic transactions. I want here to stay with the idea of *self* interest per se, not its role in bringing about modern capitalism, which I will treat at length in our next chapter. This idea projects for us a dramatic revolution of how we see the self. It sets aside the heroic and aristocratic values of the preceding times and offers us a more prosaic model of the self's virtues. It is once more in accord with the civilizing process, as studied by Norbert Elias. As he tells us, war-like and violent behavior must give way to less aristocratic ways. Another way of saying this is that we must all become bourgeois.

It is this bourgeois self, pursuing its self-interest,—in other words, how it profits most from an exchange—that serves as agent for the growth that is seen as necessary for the continued development of modernity. Only by self-assertion, in a market-disciplined manner, can the energy be found for the furtherance of the division of labor and the expansion of the market. It is this self that is the engine of modernity, the agent of the dynamic thrust forward. Moreover, miraculously, it is also a moral self, for it is pursuing the designs of Providence. In more secular terms, Smith labels what he is describing to be the work of an invisible hand, which guides men to a moral end they had not intended. In even more secular terms, he is talking about the laws of supply and demand. It is in this way that he reconciles his work in the *Theory* and in the *Wealth of Nations*.

However satisfactory Smith found his solution, most of us are still left with a self that is riven. A decade or so later, Immanuel Kant summed it up as man being an unsocial-social creature. Through all of this philosophic debate we must not lose sight of how Smith has changed the character of the modern self. It is a non-heroic, self-seeking self that in its search looks for both increased material well-being and for moral intercourse with its fellow humans through the imagined internal spectator. One part of Smith's work looks outward, to the material realm, the other inward, to the moral one. The two are really connected, for the outward as it is changed in turn changes the inward, the way we see the world we are newly constructing. It is a pair of spectacles, with its two lenses, not a Cyclopean telescope, that offers us the correct image of our modern circumstances.

In the end, self and society are constructed together. One's life is a project in this view, undertaken at the same time as the progressive development of society is an external project. A different time, and oneself would be different. By the same token, to understand anything means to understand it in the context of its historical development and of the history that presently surrounds it. The overall term to cover this view is historicism. In contrast to the unchanging scientific self of Descartes, we must now try to comprehend in depth the historicist self of a second phase of modernity (though the first phase persists alongside of it).

## (4)

The figure who best allows us to pursue this inquiry is Hegel. As a recent biography by Terry Pinkard, the most praise-worthy one now extant, argues, Hegel is "the first great philosopher to make modernity itself the object of his thought."[4] This is not surprising since, as we are further told, "no generation lived through such a wrenching transformation of ways of life as did Hegel's." It is the German philosopher's generation, experiencing both political and industrial revolutions, that derived from that experience a sense of liberation from what it came to understand as self-constructed fetters, in this case especially God. In the process, humans became aware of having an identity as a freedom-aspiring individual. At the end, these same humans took on godlike powers of creation; and what they created, according to Hegel, was history as freedom.

Descartes had already shown the way. His form of hubris was to have himself construct the universe in the same manner as God had done. This was the scientific self expanding to fill the universe and its space. Hegel's expansion was in terms of time. Man's gradual self-determination took place in the course of history, as he came closer and closer to godlike powers and comprehension. Each philosophy—Descartes's and Hegel's—can be seen as a secular outlook that draws upon the religious vision in order to displace religion and place Man in its place. Here we have one of the key attributes of the modern self: its claim to be independent and self-sufficient. It is self-made, as long as we realize that that making takes place in correlation with the society that is also being newly created.

This version of individualism stands in contrast to the traditional ties of community. I would argue that the latter is not done away with completely—that is a fantasy of Robinson Crusoe's—but is changed into a collection of other individuals. These are others in relation to whom the individual becomes him/her self. We have already seen a piece of this development in Smith's notion of the impartial spectator. It undergoes its full development and deepening in the thinking of Hegel. It reflects the long awakening through history of self-consciousness.

Hegel's modernity was to take the introspective self, as developed by Pietists, Rousseau, and Romantics, and make it self-conscious, and then send it spinning out into the world in order to rediscover itself. Self is not a stable unchanging essence, but a dialectically unfolding project. Such a self is necessarily a social self, where it can only discover its nature dialectically, and in terms of other selves and their doings. The self, in short, becomes an ongoing, historical creation, constantly being brought into being as a result of one's self's interaction with other selves and the historical consequences of such relationships.

The first part of this awareness is in terms of self-consciousness, now lifted to a new level by Hegel. As he writes, "Two things must be distinguished in consciousness; first, the fact *that I know*; secondly, *what I know*. In *self* consciousness these are merged in one; for Spirit *knows itself*. It involves an appreciation of its own nature, as also an energy enabling it to realize itself; to make itself *actually* that which it is *potentially*." This cryptic passage is given extended explication in the introduction of *The Philosophy of History* (1831), to which I will return briefly a little later.

Remaining with self-consciousness per se, for the moment, we can secure a better notion of what Hegel has in mind in the following passage. Though long and arcane, it is essential to quote it entirely. "Self-consciousness has before it another self-consciousness; it has come outside itself. This has a double significance. First, it has lost its own self, since it finds itself as an *other* being; secondly, it has thereby sublated that other, for it does not regard the other as essentially real, but sees its own self in the other." He continues, "It must cancel this its other. To do so is the sublation of that first double meaning, and is therefore a second double meaning. First, it must set itself to sublate the other independent being, in order thereby to become certain of itself as true being, secondly, it thereupon proceeds to sublate its own self, for this other is itself."[5]

One can readily see why such prose arouses annoyed feelings in most readers. What is he saying? And why can't he say it in straight English (really German)? The answer is that Hegel is working through philosophical thickets toward an original concept of the modern self and its consciousness. He is groping toward the idea. Such thinking is central to his *Phenomenology of Mind*, published in 1807, just as Napoleon's armies are massed outside of Jena, where Hegel is writing, and where the full force of his reconception of the self is set forth. The result is the historicist/modern self of his century, and beyond. This self insists on recognizing itself in terms of an *other* self, in some ways its double, but yet different. Such difference, however, must be struggled against and with in order to realize one's own selfhood—which turns out to be that of humanity's at large. At this point, the other and one's self merge, parts of the same historical process.

A paradigmatic example of what Hegel has in mind is the master-slave relation. A more or less universal form of relation, while it persists the master cannot achieve true self-consciousness, for the slave who is his other is not allowed to have such a consciousness and thereby be a true other for the master. The slave can provide his master with labor and its fruits, but not a true self. Only through a dialectical development in which the master-slave distinction is transcended can real self-consciousness be realized. Such dialectic is not only in the mind, but in the historical world. Hegel was writing (I owe this insight to Susan Buck-Morss) at a time when, inspired by the events of 1789, the Haitian Revolution of 1803 had temporarily succeeded. Changes in the mind—increased self-consciousness—and changes in society, mediated through mind, were parts of one process.

In achieving his transforming leap, I would claim, Hegel actually started from Descartes's rational ego. But the German philosopher conceptualized reason as developing through experience, becoming conscious of itself as it builds the outside world. By experience, however, Hegel does not mean scientific encounters with empirical reality but the progress of what he calls Idea, Spirit, or Mind through history. As he seeks to show in detail in his *Philosophy of History*, reason realizes itself over time and through successive dialectical stages. Only at the moment when the owl of Minerva takes flight—that is, only when the past is known to us in the present, the *just now* of the modern, can the modern self see the path that Spirit has taken up to this point.

Even then it is only a temporary resting point. The restless self and Spirit are engaged in a dialectical development that ever moves forward. We have seen some of the elements that form part of that dialectic: Bacon's empiricism, Descartes's deductive reason, Smith's impartial spectator and self-interested profiteer, Hegel's self-conscious and historicist Reason. To these we must now add the notion of an affective revolution.

As one author puts it, "Sentiment, not reason, was the great social invention of the second half of the eighteenth century. . . . [S]entiment was nothing less than modernity."[6] Partly this was because sentiment was seen as the basis of sociability rather more than was reason. Such sociability was rooted in human nature. Individuals, in this view, are linked together in society by feeling more than by a social contract arrived at by reasoning beings. Quite specifically, Smith's teacher Francis Hutcheson equated moral feelings, such as benevolence, with aesthetic responses: both are spontaneous reactions to what we experience in our everyday life, built into our being human.

Two comments are required. The first is that we need not choose between sentiment and reason as the cause of modernity: both are required. The second is that sentiment tends to get neglected because no great name, leaving aside perhaps Rousseau and to a much lesser degree Hutcheson, is attached to it; the author cited above refers to Henry Mackenzie. Nevertheless, the history of the emotions must be studied as much as that of reason. It enters into the modern mentality arm in arm with the latter. As another author tells us, in the "affective revolution, each sensitive heart recognizes simultaneously its own emotions and those of its secret sharer."[7]

We easily recognize the Hegelian modality in this last statement. We become conscious about our reasoning self and our affective self through the same process of playing them off against other such selves. Hegel himself, though he does not particularly deal with the emotions in his own account of the rise of self-consciousness, does recognize in his *Philosophy of History* the central role of the passions. He had read his Adam Smith to good purpose, and saw that the sordid ambitions of man was the fuel pushing Man toward Reason. Together, we can conclude, sentiment and reason conspired to bring about modernity.

(5)

And the modern self. This self is a contested self, in which many forces are at play and war. I have tried to describe these forces as building on the seeing revolution, which manifested itself so vigorously in the scientific revolution of the seventeenth century and then worked itself into the cultural and social fabric of the times. Thus, a major part of the modern self is one that sees scientifically. Such a way of seeing, what we have come to call scientific method, is a compound of empiricism and rationalism. Symbolized in the figures of Bacon and Descartes, it is an essential part of any modern self, then and now.

Alongside of the scientific component of the modern self, we must then place the divided self projected for us by Adam Smith and Hegel. Smith's emphasis was on both the moral self and the economic self, on the famous impartial spectator lurking within each of us and on the infamous self-interested drive behind our actions in exchange relations. Hegel then added depth to the notion of the moral self by exploring how it becomes self-conscious in the presence of an other. He then inquired into its relation with the historical development of the species, correlating the one with the other. Though Hegel's treatment was idealistic; in terms of abstractions such as the Idea, or Spirit, others could take his insight in a more empirical (even materialistic) direction.

Lastly, I noted the sentimental journey of the modern self. It must figure in any historicist portrait of that self. As can readily be seen, the self has broken loose from its ties to traditional community and belief and been made to stand on its own, individual feet, so to speak. The larger term for this development is individualism. It encompasses the way in which the self has emancipated itself from a previous existence—a premodern existence—characterized by feudal notions and relations and a monopolistic, mercantile constriction of trade and commerce (to be examined further in our next chapter).

While I have tried to get at the features of the modern self emerging in the seventeenth through eighteenth centuries by means of representative thinkers, that self was to be found in ordinary people in the society of the time. In other words, society and self were becoming modern together. Single thinkers, such as Smith or Hegel, embody parts of that self and figure it forth in intellectual terms, which is why they are so useful as guides to the complex reality around them. And insofar as modernity consists of a momentous shift in consciousness, one that occurred first and foremost in Western Europe (and to an extent in America), it is fitting to proceed in the terms I have. I need only add that what I have described can be called an ideal type, to which would then have to be added the material changes (some of which I will touch on in the next chapter) going on at the time in order to have a truer composite picture.

Is there a unity to the modern self, as I have described it? I think that the answer is yes, but not in the traditional way. The unity of the modern self is made up of the contestation and splintering that enter into its existence. In this, it is true to the very insights that have been achieved by the self as it emerges into modern times. This is, however, a unity that is not felt by the self experiencing it. The experience of the self is as a divided being, pulled in many different directions, and with differential force, toward a goal only dimly sensed. Thus, our lived sensibilities, later to be labeled with the philosophical designation of phenomenology, pull us apart, leaving us confused and divided. It is only as seen by historical reason that the modern self can be viewed as having a unity. It is one of direction and possible purpose in a constantly expanding and eventually evolving world, not of an essence. Such a self—scientific, historicist, and both moral and self-seeking—is adapted to the modern society and culture it is creating. It may not be a happy or perfectly adjusted self, but it is one conscious of its condition. It is therefore potentially aware of the ways in which it might change both itself and the modern world.

Among these ways is to recognize the changing nature of labor and the role of work in the world. It is by working, utilizing the division of labor, which allows for increased productivity aligned with an expanding market, that the modern self can create a world after its own heart and reason. That world has come to be called capitalism. It is to capitalism that we now turn in our next chapter.

## Notes

1.  Jacob Burckhardt, *The Civilization of the Renaissance in Italy* (Phaidon Press, 1945), 81.

2.  Ernst Cassirer, *The Individual and the Cosmos in Renaissance Philosophy* (Chicago Press, 2010), 35.

3.  Francis Bacon, "Advancement of Learning." In:Timothy Dwight et al., *The World's Great Classics* (New York: The Colonial Press, 1899), 105.

4.  Pinkard, Terry, *Hegel. A Biography* (Cambridge University Press, 2000), x.

5.  G.W.F. Hegel, *The Phenomenology of Mind*, transl. by J. B. Baillie (Harper Torchbooks, 1967), 229.

6.  James Buchan, *Crowded with Genius – The Scottish Enlightenment: Edinburgh's Moment of the Mind* (Harper Collins, 2003), 302.

7.  DeJean, op. cit., 123.

# 4

# The Capitalist Society

In the previous chapter, we have seen how a scientific and aesthetic modern self emerged over the course of a few centuries. Now we must examine another aspect of the modern self: its *self*-interested capitalist nature.

Capital as such seems always to have existed. Farming tools, no matter how primitive, can be so considered if effort is required to produce them, and they are at least moderately durable. (A stone picked up to throw at a potential meal would not be; a flint arrowhead would.) But capitalist *society* is a different matter, a late and complicated development. It appears to approach domination in the West in the form of commercial capitalism around the seventeenth century. By the nineteenth century, in the form of industrial capitalism, it has come to dominate much of the world. It is important to remember that the very notion of society is a seventeenth-century idea, occurring at the same time as the so-called scientific revolution. Thus, we should now add the capitalist self to the scientific self we discussed in the previous chapter. Both in its beginning and dominance, the capitalist self was not always admired. Martin Luther declared that capitalists should be broken on the wheel. Presumably he had in mind usurers, those who lent money at interest (often exorbitant) and were despised in both Christian and Islamic societies. Subsequent to capitalism's success in shaping society, it gave rise in the nineteenth century to socialism, which wished to abolish or at least to rein in capitalism's growing influence.

Capitalism means the accumulation of capital so as to invest it in order to profit and thus increase the capital to be once again invested. Dynamism is built into the system. Karl Marx described it brilliantly, in the *Communist Manifesto*, as a werewolf appetite. It takes a certain type of personality to think and work in capitalist terms. Previous economies had in mind such goals as setting a just price, not the price the commodity would bear as a result of supply and demand.

The notion and reality of society had as its counterpart the notion and realty of the individual. This meant a private self, though embedded in a community. Material life, as Fernand Braudel has pointed out, reflected and helped further develop this sense of a private self. As he also pointed out, "Capitalism, with its rules, attitudes, advantages and risks, has betokened modernity, flexibility and rationality from its earliest beginnings."[1] It is all of a piece. The scientific, the capitalist, and the modern self all cohered.

Trade has existed for eons. By the time of the seventeenth century in the West, however, historians can speak of a commercial revolution and commercial society. Such economic activity led to efforts to theorize about it. Thus, pamphlets and treatises on banking, currency, and credit appeared as practical guides to commercial activity. Only in the eighteenth century do we find efforts to see the economy as a total system and to try to analyze it rationally.[2]

The initial effort was made by the Physiocrats. A sort of sect, led by François Quesnay, they took their name from their attempt to be ruled by nature. Physiocrats believed that land was wealth; all other things, such as manufacturing and trade, were mere transformations of that original production. Hence it followed that tax should be laid solely upon the produce of the land.

Quesnay also introduced the idea of an *annual* circulation of production, an idea that has persisted until this day. He also propagated the virtues of *laissez-faire, laissez-passer*. At a time in France when it is estimated that goods going from one end of the country to another would have to pay tolls at almost four hundred stations, this was an understandable cri de coeur.

Adam Smith was very respectful of the Physiocrats, visiting France to talk to them, but he shifted the definition of wealth from land to labor. It was the division of labor that was the motor of progress, the latter a very popular idea at the time. We have already in the previous chapter described both Smith's moral and economic ideas at greater length. Here I want to emphasize his justification of the desire for profit as part of an acquisitive self. Situated in a capitalist society, it is a self whose desire to innovate and accumulate is at one with the scientific self whose nature we have delineated earlier.

For Smith the only limit to the division of labor was the extent of the market. And the capitalist self with its ceaseless dynamism had extended its tentacles to the whole world. The highest paean to this process was written by Marx (who can be seen as the last of the classical economists) and Engels in the *Communist Manifesto*. As they remark, "Modern industry has established the world market, for which the discovery of America paved the way. This market has given an immense development to commerce, to navigation, to communication by land." Indeed, to make my point I should probably reproduce the entire *Manifesto* here.

The main point is to see that the notion of society, and the various selves that have been described, are all cohering.

For our discussion we need to make one other extension of this multiple self. It is the emphasis on the individual. Seeking to identify the difference or similarity between the notions of the self and the individual, we must accept the fact that there is much ambiguity and overlap. The self appears to be closer to the community, willing to take part in the latter's activities. The term *individual* suggests a greater aloofness. Reified, we can speak of individualism. It requires the idea of society in order to play off against itself. This antithesis has been expressed in numerous ways, from Kant's social/antisocial nature of man to later sociological formulations of *Gemeinschaft* und *Gesellschaft* to the debate over community and the individual. (As we saw in a previous chapter, this had already been foreshadowed in the battle of the ancients and the moderns.)

Novels, a prominent feature of the modern, can often be as revealing as more official documents. Thus, in her novel about Turkey, *The Sultan's Seal*, the anthropologist Jenny White has written how "In the East, people were first and foremost members of their family, their tribe, their community. Their own desires were irrelevant; the solidarity and survival of the group paramount. Selfishness couldn't occur because there were no selves, only fathers and sons, mothers and daughters, husbands and wives."[3] What a different world from that of Adam Smith and its dynamic self and self-expansion!

As noted before, self-criticism is an integral part of the modern and scientific self. Thus, both antimodernity and anticapitalism have flourished at the same time as their targets have been expanding. Such antagonistic feelings often took the form of art. Max Weber had spoken of modernity's "disenchantment of the world." He meant that all things were now viewed rationally, with the air, so to speak, being emptied of angels. His insight was only partial. The other aspect of modernity was its aestheticism of the world, where everything was seen under the form of art.

Increasingly, such art joined the rational form of capitalist expansion in the form of consumerism. One historian has written of the birth of consumer society, dating it from the eighteenth century on.[4] As is well known, by the twentieth century this was further promoted by the employment of advertising. At this time, too, both capitalism and its ally, advertising, had gone global.

For the pluralistic person of the present, the scientific, capitalist, and aesthetic parts of his or her personality coexist and cohere. Of course, the appearance of such a *persona* is differentiated across the world. At the same time, capitalism itself metamorphoses from commercial to industrial to financial capitalism. In each of these embodiments, various classes emerge into prominence, such as a bourgeoisie, industrial workers, service-sector employees, and those who handle only money and credit.

At the end of the nineteenth century, in the developed countries, science was put to work steadily in the service of technology. Technology in the new chemical and electrical industries that were emerging in what has been called a second Industrial Revolution is a prime example. These, with the iron and steel processes developed in the early phase of the Industrial Revolution, along with the mechanized textile industry, and then the innovation of the steam engine and the railroad in the first half of the nineteenth century, gave a power and speed to the modern world hitherto unknown. With the advent of the telegraph in the middle of the century, the speed of communication took a great leap forward.

All this, and more, is a well-known story. I repeat it here in order to make vivid the way a world market had come into being along with the tools by which to manufacture the products that now were carried to all parts of the world. We are well beyond the sixteenth- to seventeenth-century search for spices from the Far East in exchange for silver and textiles from the West. Somewhere in this story belongs the steamship, which in the nineteenth century displaced the sailing cutters of the China trade and elsewhere, allowing people to move across the oceans in a more predictable way.

Such is the prolegomena of modernity, especially in its economic aspects, opening the way to its correlation with and replacement by post–World War II globalization. In a sense, one can say that modernity and antimodernity combined to commit suicide, first in the Great War of 1914–1918, and then in the truly worldwide Second War of 1939–1945. Developments emanating from that Second War and its resulting Cold War prepared the way for the rupture that resulted in globalization.[5]

Thus, we must notice the development of the rocket foreshadowing the satellites that fostered the computer revolution that was to come. Much tied up with the decipherment of codes, the computer dated back to the first half of the nineteenth century, when Charles Babbage invented and built his difference engine (which one must see, I believe, as part of the first Industrial Revolution). Its development was only vigorously resumed in the course of World War II. Thence it exploded in terms of the personal computer, the web, and the Internet.

We tend to need and to emphasize the continuity of life in order to have a sense of stability. Yet, more and more, the pace of life has quickened. This was true of modernity, with its ceaseless pursuit of the new and what it saw as progress. I will claim that this pace of change has not only been retained in globalization but has again accelerated. It is why I argue for its being a rupture. The reasons why I so argue are to be found in the next chapter.

# Notes

1.  Fernand Braudel, *Capitalism and Material Life 1400–1800* (Harper, 1973), xiii.
2.  See especially William Letwin, *The Origins of Scientific Economic Thought, 1660–1776* (Routledge, 2003), and Joyce Appleby, *Ideology and Economic Thought in Seventeenth-Century England* (Princeton, 1978).
3.  Jenny White, *The Sultan's Seal* (2006), 230.
4.  Neil McKendrick, John Brewer and J. H. Plumb, *The Birth of a Consumer Society. The Commercialization of Eighteenth-century England* (Europea Publications Limited, London, 1982).
5.  See further Bruce Mazlish, *The New Global History* (Routledge, 2006), Chapter 3.

# 5

# Globalization: A Rupture

Globalization is by now a clearly acknowledged phenomenon. What exactly that phenomenon is, however, is a
hotly debated question. The term itself achieves currency,
it appears, sometime in the 1950s, and widespread usage by
the 1970s. Its definition emphasizes that it means increased
interconnectivity and interdependence among peoples and
societies. Once the concept has been formed, it can then
be extended retroactively to the past. Thus, globalization
can be said to have been taking place from the time of the
hunter-gatherers to the present. It is as if Moliere's *bourgeois
gentilhomme* suddenly realized he has been speaking prose.

How best can we understand what is going on? Peoples
everywhere need to divide up the past in understandable
ways. Often using the moon as a marker, they construct
calendars of some sort. With the coming of civilizations,
division by dynasties became the marker, with later historians also constructing kingdoms to set off different periods.
Thus, present-day scholars talk about Old, Middle, and New
Kingdoms in Egypt. With the coming of Christianity, we
have the widely accepted BC/AD. Islam then arrives with
its own calendar. By the time of the Renaissance—another
timely rubric—the notion of ancient, medieval, and modern

history emerged—one that is still largely with us, and has spread from the West to the rest of the globe. Somewhere around the seventeenth century, we have the idea of an *age*, as in the age of Louis XIV. With the French Revolution of 1789, we have the end of dynastic periodization, although the word *Age* has hung around. These periodizations can be misused badly. For example, to speak of medieval Islam is really to mean Islam at the time of the European middle ages; they are not the middle ages in the Islamic world.

Given this background, we must remind ourselves that historians generally work on the assumption that the past is both continuous and discontinuous. Stringing together facts, in what is implied to be a deterministic way, a smooth line is drawn through the past. Both the facts and the continuity are, we now realize, constructed. We construct what is a fact, and could have emphasized other ones, and we impose the continuity upon those we have selected. In similar fashion, historians also construct discontinuities, in order to deal with such happenings as the French Revolution of 1789 and, more latterly, post–World War II globalization.

Let us look carefully at *ruptures*, *breaks* and *turning points*, terms used by historians to deal with what they see as major discontinuities. All three terms have overlapping meanings. They are permeable to one another. Thus, there is bound to be a vagueness in their definitions. The French Revolution, for example, is widely recognized as a rupture. Nevertheless, Alexis de Tocqueville wrote his book on the old regime emphasizing the Revolution's continuity with the past. Less convincingly, Arno Mayer wrote a book, *The Persistence of the Old Regime* (1981), arguing that the power of the aristocracy as an elite largely persisted into the nineteenth century.

Let us examine further the three terms. As I remarked, they have overlapping meanings, but a common core. Rupture, in an old-fashioned dictionary, *Webster's New Collegiate Dictionary*

(1974), is defined as coming through the Latin to a French word meaning to break. Not surprisingly, there is no allusion to history. If one looks up rupture on Google, one finds that it is mostly defined in geological or medical terms. The historical we must work out for ourselves. I suggest that we think of it as a major cut in the continuity of the past. It is the strongest of our three terms.

There is, of course, the matter of differences, often subtle, in our three terms. *Break* seems the least significant. We speak of a break in sports events. A break can often mean a new chance. In regard to history, we speak of a break with traditions. It is generally an indeterminate term, and gives us limited understanding of what is alleged to have happened.

*Turning point* seems to offer more specificity. There is an assumption that we are on a path that can be reasonably well described, as to where it is coming from and in what direction it seems to be proceeding. Then something happens to turn it from its presumed path. A related word—watershed—is frequently found alongside, which carries a different valence.

Of course, all our terms, and we should include *revolution*, remind us of the contingent and dynamic nature of historical experience. Against the view of the human past as marked by continuity, they represent abrupt changes. There is for the historian always a tension between continuity and discontinuity. For the latter, the term *rupture* appears the best to help us comprehend that the events under consideration consist of endings as well as beginnings. (The overtones of *rapture* are also worth attention.)

Some usages are of a minor nature, others of major significance. Among the former, we are told that "Naval combat as it had been fought for millennia does appear to have changed after 1945."[1] We can no longer envision battles of Midway in the future. Combat between huge Dreadnoughts seem a thing of the past. Surely, this is a rupture with the past, even if a minor one.

I want to mention two more ruptures that I consider more significant for the way they point to the future. The first is what I call the judicial revolution. Though of course with predecessors, it can be dated as emerging in post–World War II times. It starts with the Nuremberg trials of 1945-46, and with two important assertions made in the course of the prosecution. One is that war itself is a crime. Earlier there was recognition of war crimes—that is, crimes committed during a war. Now war itself was asserted to be a crime. Here we are at a major rupture in the history of military conflict.

The second assertion was that the Nazis and their allies had committed crimes against humanity. Genocide was the most prominent, but other actions were also so labeled. The 1946 trial was quickly followed by those of Yugoslavia and Rwanda. The International Criminal Court has been the last so far of these legal innovations. Whatever problems in implementation, and there have been many, the principle was established that those who committed either war crimes or crimes against humanity were subject to international jurisdiction, unrestrained by appeals to national sovereignty. Here, indeed, is a rupture in the domain of international law.

I believe that an even more consequential development emerged, and is emerging. If there are crimes against humanity, the question arises: what is this humanity that has been sinned against? It is with this query that the concept of Humanity, as a new identity on top of the local and the national, emerges. The idea had existed in the heads of philosophers before, in the clouds so to speak. Now it was appearing in real life. As such it took on actual shape because of globalization and the communications revolution. By means of the latter, fostered by computers and satellites that allowed for instant communication anywhere, an unprecedented compression of space and time took place. All this potentially fosters the development of the concept of Humanity as a true sovereign body, whose voice should constantly be heard and whose presence leads to the transcending of national sovereignty.

Of course, this does not take place easily, and its outcome is not determined. The push back of national sovereignty is powerful. As the saying goes, though the global is everywhere, even in the local, all politics is local. To the national we must then add the increasing presence and force of what can be called ethno-politics. Today, ethno-politics—often expressed in the form of terrorism, appealing to ethno and religious politics rather than nationalism as in the past—has molded warfare into a new shape (though the War on Terror was a monumental mistake in naming), with global reach.

This takes us back to the other major rupture of our time, in my view the most significant and far-reaching, both for today and in the future. It is the coming of globalization. The topic, as it should, often evokes heated passion, ranging from acknowledgment that it exists, but is detested—antiglobalization—to a denial that it is anything new, worth evoking the term rupture.

Let me continue to make the case for its being a most significant rupture, a truly tectonic shift. Worthy of note is that the term globalization itself is a coinage of the period, emerging sometime in the 1950s through the1980s, and gaining widespread currency. Once in existence it could then be applied to prewar history. Of course, globalization existed from the beginning, with prehistoric man roaming across Earth.

The globalization into which we inquire now is different. After World War II, with the coming and spread of computers and satellites, the increased interconnectivity and interdependency of Homo sapiens was unparalleled. Time and space were compressed beyond compare, in real time. Thus, you the reader and I the writer can communicate immediately. I can do this with my neighbor in Russia or China as quickly as

I can with the family next door in person. The consequences are enormous.

As is so frequently stated, many of our most important problems now are of a global nature, transgressing the borders of existing nation-states and regions. Climate change, though passionately debated, is surely one. So is the ecological exhaustion of much of the earth, pushed forward by economic exploitation.

Political, social, and cultural consequences are of equal importance. Increasing integrations of states, such as the European Union, mark a regional advance, with the resultant federation then able to deal with the challenges of globalization in a more unified fashion. In this same union, passport controls have been abolished and freedom of movement instituted, at least in principle. Peoples occupy a much more common social space.

To my eyes, the two most significant and long-range effects of globalization as I have already emphasized are global consciousness—that is, being aware everywhere of being on one globe—and the emergence of the concept of Humanity. Five million people across the globe, it is claimed, saw the first moon landing in real time and at the same time. Millions and millions more have now heard of global climate change, and must think of (if only to deny) its effect on their local condition. Viewing the planet Earth from outer space, and images like the brilliant dymaxion map by Buckminster Fuller have made us aware in unprecedented fashion of the fact that we all inhabit one Earth. Such consciousness is a rupture in our previous state of awareness.

At this point, further questions arise. Are ruptures in our history growing more and more frequent? Are they larger ruptures than previously, perhaps because of globalization as a rupture? Can ruptures be predicted? Are peoples more conscious of them because of globalization and its concomitant communications revolution?

Another set of questions concerns the political implications involved in privileging the notion of rupture. Conservatives, almost by definition, tend to prefer continuity. As Edmund Burke classically argued, reform should come gradually, whereas revolution rends the entire fabric of society. Ruptures, or in this case actually a revolution, more or less puts an end to an old regime. Some decades after 1789, Thomas Carlyle spoke of the Industrial Revolution as ending feudal society and preparing the way for industrial society. Certainly, that ending had seen its prelude in the fall of the Bastille. In short, views about revolutions and ruptures are profoundly political.

Hitherto, most historians have generally seen the past in terms of continuity, as a continuous plain, occasionally interrupted by hills and volcanoes. What I am proposing is that historians will do better in understanding the past, especially the recent past, as being in the shape of a series of hills and volcanoes (which occasionally erupt), with flat plains interspersed among them. This entails a shift in our mental landscape to a globalscape, a Copernican revolution of sorts. It suggests a different mindset. Historiography itself will thus be experiencing a rupture.

I am arguing that we gain much greater understanding by looking at globalization as a rupture that opens up after World War II. What are some of the factors that compose the process, or processes, of globalization, for we must make what is involved concrete and subject to further research?

During the war, rocketry was much developed. In fact, an earlier predecessor was the Russian scientist Konstantin Tsiolkovsky, who in 1903 published his exploration of the principles involved. On this basis came the artificial satellites (the moon is a natural one) that so distinguish our era. The first launch into space was the Russian Sputnik in 1957. This was an Earth-orbiting satellite, and it triggered a space arms race between the Soviet Union and the United States.

Subsequently, hundreds and hundreds of satellites were launched by both superpowers, with thousands floating around as debris. Next followed launches that went beyond the Earth's atmosphere into outer space. One of the most dramatic was sending a spaceship to the moon, where the astronauts could collect rock samples and bring them back to Earth (so much for the green cheese theory!).

On Earth itself, meanwhile, a computer revolution was taking place. Harking back to Charles Babbage and his difference engine, actually built in 1832, the computer developed from huge mainframes into personal computers. These small versions, able to be held on one's lap, were each more powerful than all previous devices. Able to allow communication with one another, they formed an internet, as well as a world wide web.

Such technological advances fostered the process of globalization, bringing humankind to greater interconnectivity and interdependence. This is just as well because our problems are increasingly global. Many are caused by the processes of globalization, conjuring up antiglobalization movements. Yet, it is only by further globalization, connected to the concept of Humanity, that humans can meet the challenges of global problems. Given the stubbornness of national forces, it will hardly be a smooth development. Indeed, Humanity may never develop, remaining stunted forever. I do not believe in predetermined ends in history. Yet, human intervention in this world of indeterminacy is a moral requirement, with possible good effects in this world itself. Globalization, with its concomitant of the concept of Humanity, is definitely on the agenda of the human species.

### Note

1.    John T. Kuehn, "Is Mahan Dead?" *Historically Speaking*, vol. XII (1), (January 2011), 30.

# 6

# Periodizing Globalization

As M. I. Finley, the great scholar of antiquity, put it, "Dates and a coherent dating system are as essential to history as exact measurement is to physics."[1] Such a view justifies the current effort to periodize globalization. The process of globalization in the sense of hunter-gatherers moving and migrating around the world, later to be seen as a globe, has deep roots in the past. Yet to best understand the process requires us to start from the present.

That present starts with post–World War II developments. First, we must glance at the Nuremberg Trials of 1945–1946. In its pursuit of crimes against humanity it identified all peoples as one. With the Rwandan and Yugoslav trials, followed by the establishment of an International Criminal Court, the rights of humanity were extended and expanded. Thus the ideal of a common humanity across the globe was given real substance.

This globalization of justice was matched by a growing *consciousness* of the process of globalization itself. All peoples were involved in the process both as agents and as individuals being acted upon, both singularly and collectively. This awareness was sharply increased by two events. One was Hiroshima, which the sociologist Martin Albrow called "the first global event,"[2] and which thus marked the transition from modernity to globalization. That nuclear explosion made it clear that all of humanity and its achievements might be destroyed by mushroom clouds. The second event was the landing on the moon, where Armstrong uttered the famous words (or some version of) "That's one small step for [a] man, one giant leap for mankind." (No matter that he then planted an American flag in the rocky soil.)

To find the first manifestation of globalization, however, we must probably go back two hundred thousand years, to the hunter-gatherer-scavengers who were the ancestors of Homo sapiens. Here in small groups—numbering probably no more than forty to fifty—they wondered across the world. This can be called the *first* period of globalization.

Before going further we should note the work of Reinhart Koselleck, calling into question the entire project of periodization. Though controversy surrounds the issue of how to interpret his views, a strong argument can be made that the esteemed German historian "challenges and even defies periodization." In a very penetrating article, Helge Jordheim argues that Koselleck developed "his theory of multiple temporalities, organized in the form of temporal layers that have different origin and duration and move at different speeds, as an alternative to the linear and empty time of periodization."[3]

This is a powerful argument and must give us pause. However, it does not, in my view, invalidate the usefulness of periodization; it only qualifies it. There must be classification as humans seek to impose order on their experiences. Geologists speak of Pleistocene and other periods to give us a greater manipulable grasp of prehistoric times. As long as we recognize the constructed nature of these periodizations we are safe in using them.

A valuable contribution on the nature of our problem is the book[4] *The Course of Human History*, especially the first chapter by Johan Goudsblom. He concentrates on what he feels is the most important organizing principle for history: chronology. This is at first usually expressed in terms of monarchies and dynasties. Then impersonal stages of phases are substituted. Phaseology is substituted for chronology. A phase model is not inherently place-bound, but applicable to humanity at large. At this point we can talk about long-term processes and turning points. A final step is to identify dominant trends.

With these highly suggestive ideas of Koselleck and Goudsblom in mind, we can return to our own attempt at the periodizing of globalization. A few preliminary statements are required. First, of course, is the very definition of globalization. A. G. Hopkins describes it as involving "the extension, intensification and quickening velocity of flows of people, products and ideas that shape the world. It integrates regions and continents. The results alter and may even transform relationships within and among states and societies across the globe."[5] Others emphasize the accelerated compression of time and space. Essential seems the increased interconnectivity and interdependency of peoples.

Next we must constantly bear in mind that globalization operates at different rates, with different effects in different parts of the world. In addition, it gives rise to antiglobalization, which manifests itself often in discontinuous form. It is not even clear whether globalization will continue to increase, or suffer reverses or even a disappearance (unlikely, in my view). Global effects, such as climate change or ecological exhaustion, may wipe out globalization itself.

One last preliminary note. There are at least three other attempts by distinguished scholars to deal with our subject. They are worth mentioning here, and not just as footnotes. One is Bernard Lewis, "The Periodization of History— Excerpts," a talk given at the Gatestone Institute on February

16, 2009. His presentation has the special advantage of looking at the subject as much in regard to Islamic culture as European. For example, the "Middle Ages" cannot be applied automatically to Muslim countries; it makes no sense.

The second attempt is by the pioneering world historian and editor of *The Journal of World History*, Jerry Bentley. In an article in the *American Historical Review* he proposes "cross cultural interactions–the participation of the world's peoples in processes that transcend individual societies and cultural regions–as a foundation for just such a periodization." On this basis he argues for six major periods. In the first, "migration and trade promoted the diffusion of horse domestication and bronze metallurgy."[6] The second, although oddly he doesn't actually use that term, is characterized by bronze technology and migration and trade. A "third period of global history" is the age of classical civilizations. A fourth era of global history "which for lack of a better term" he calls the "post-classical age." A fifth is an age of trans-regional interactions, especially characterized by the actions of nomadic peoples. A sixth era of world history extends from the fifteenth century to the present and is marked by peoples' sustained interaction so as to inaugurate a genuinely global epoch of world history.

Patrick Manning is a kindred spirit to Bentley, and also a leading figure in world history. His *Narrating World History* has become a classic textbook. He endorses Bentley's periodization, but in discussing ways of constructing periods he suggests going beyond trade and migration and bringing in food crops, dress, and family structure.

Important and major as the contributions of Bentley and Manning are, I am troubled by what I see as their imperial reach; by that I mean their attempt to encompass all of the past and other emphases in history. They seem insensitive to other structurings, such as global and new global history.

Indeed, as a part of their reach they sometimes use *world* and *global* as synonyms. They ignore the fact that after World War II there is what I call a rupture in globalization, marked as it is by the term globalization itself being coined and coming into common currency. It is a major shift in consciousness, made vivid to millions by the moon landing. I believe that recognizing this rupture, and then looking back into the past, has great heuristic value.

Many historians either ignore or disdain the sociology of knowledge. I believe that it gives us valuable insights of a special kind. Using this lens we can see that there are at least two major reasons for the rise and spread of world history. First, it responds to the laudable desire to transcend Eurocentrism. Next it allows everyone to get into the act, and to bring in from the periphery their own field of concentration. Thus, while Bentley began in European Renaissance history, thus weakening my thesis, Manning's roots are in African history. Needless to say, we must not make too much of what is said here.

Let us return to our line of argument. We can now conceive of all of past human history as a dissolution of the first phase of globalization, its breakdown into particular forms of social bonding, and then the reassembly or at least drive to a state of global humanity. The forms of social bonding take the famous stadial form announced especially by Scottish philosophers of the eighteenth century such as Adam Ferguson and Adam Smith. (Parenthetically, it is a delicious tidbit to note that both men leading their contemporaries to a greater awareness of globalization were named Adam.) They saw the stages of human association as moving from the family to the clan, the tribe, empires, and nation-states.

Stepping back from that vision for the moment, we can return to what I will label the *second* period of globalization. It arises in terms of what has been called the axial revolution, when the great monotheistic religions with their assertions of universality first began to emerge. Such religions were intended to encompass the entire globe. At about the same time, around the fifth century BC, we witness the appearance of the great Ionian and Greek thinkers. They too thought in global terms, their ideas projected as having universal validity. Reason was the same everywhere.

Among these thinkers we find Herodotus, the father of history, exploring a step into a realm beyond myth, where rational inquiry could guide us. He assumed the universality of human experience. He was writing the history of the Greco-Persian wars, but also a universal history. Thucydides, his successor, assumed that man was everywhere basically the same and that therefore the past held lessons for all peoples, everywhere and for all time.

We must remember what for them constituted the universe. They had no awareness of another continental mass to their West. They were not sure that the world was a globe. It is true that Eratosthenes in the fifth-century BC calculated the circumference of the globe at around twenty-nine thousand miles, strikingly close to present-day calculations, but his view of a globe was not widely known or accepted. Thus, this second period of globalization had what must be considered a very qualified notion of the globe. Half of that sphere was, in fact, missing. Of at least equal importance was the lack of what we will call consciousness of a globe.

Before going further we must note the existence of Chinese astronomy. It was far advanced. Indeed, the Chinese in the course of their five-thousand-year civilization seemed far advanced in all fields. Perhaps one recalls Sgt. Murphy who in World War II was everywhere; the same can be said of the Chinese: mention any subject and they have been there, first. Yet, as a great Continental mass the Chinese turned inward, away from the sea. Symbolic of this fact is the story of Zheng He. Admiral of a great fleet, he was called back from his voyage to the South Seas as China turned inward. Geography and demography were destiny. Located where it was, and with almost all its needs satisfied internally, China had no need to look elsewhere.

It was left to the Western nations to venture toward a new world. Spurred on by the missionary impulses of a universal Christianity, and goaded further by greed (though one must also add curiosity), the small and weak nations of the Atlantic Coast sponsored adventurers who boldly sailed around the Cape and west to America, as it subsequently became known. Ironically, Columbus thought that he was going to reach China by sea. Surely, this was one of the most providential and productive errors in history.

It forms also what I call the *third* period of globalization. It is coincident with the European Renaissance of the fourteenth to sixteenth centuries. This is an extraordinary period. It is when an old world, classical antiquity, is resurrected, and a new world, the globe, is revealed. This period embodies Hegel's maxim that it is necessary to "reculer pour mieux sauter." The result is an almost unprecedented explosion of thought and feeling, not to mention material goods. Not only are hitherto unknown others discovered, but a new man emerges in Western Europe. A novel idea of what it means to be human inspires the countries bordering the Atlantic Ocean and then spreads elsewhere. It is the idea of an autonomous human being, able to explore and develop his own resources as well as those in other lands.

A landmark date is 1507. It was then that Martin Waldseemuller, a humanist, scholar and cartographer, produced his mind-blowing world map. One of its features was to introduce the name America as a designation of the Western Hemisphere. Its major importance, however, was to depict the entire world as a globe. As a part of the recovery of classical knowledge, Ptolemy's *Geographiae* had been rediscovered earlier; indeed, after creating his own map, Waldseemuller prepared a 1513 edition of the *Geographiae*, with its claim that Earth was the center of the universe with the sun rotating around it—a claim that generally prevailed until the epic work of Copernicus.

Equipped with the cartographic knowledge provided by Waldseemuller and others, Ferdinand Magellan sailed around the world in 1519-1521 (himself dying on the voyage), crossing into the Pacific Ocean from the Atlantic Ocean via the tip of South America. Now in the logs of his boat lay the proof that, indeed, the world was a sphere—a globe. This conquest in reality of what previously had only been in the imagination is made manifest in numerous paintings of the period showing a globe sitting on a desk. An iconic example is the painting of two ambassadors (1523) by Hans Holbein the Younger, in which a globe sits prominently in the back left hand part of the picture.

It is harder to nail down in time the *fourth* period of globalization. It occupies the long seventeenth century, whose concept also shows the wobbliness of the entire demarcation by centuries. It results mainly from mental rather than material springs. Often labeled the scientific revolution by subsequent generations, it is symbolized by the names of Kepler, Galileo, and especially Newton. Their work establishes the claim to universality of knowledge—its globalization. Both the method and its findings are valid everywhere.

With the astonishing successes of the scientific method in the natural sciences it was assumed that that method could be extended to the human sciences. The social sciences were consciously called into existence at the time of the French Revolution of 1789. Of course, work under different names had been appearing earlier. For example, pamphlets on trade, currency and so on had been written and widely circulated;

now in the late eighteenth century political economy was introduced as a formal subject, first by the Physiocrats surrounding Quesnay and then with a giant step forward by Adam Smith and his fellow workers. Thus it was proclaimed that the laws of the free market, like the laws of gravity, held everywhere. Knowledge was global.

Meanwhile a *fifth* period of globalization was being spun into existence by what we call the Industrial Revolution (thereby matching the Scientific). It took off in the late eighteenth century, when British spinning factories, iron foundries, and steam engines were central, and then developed into a second phase at the end of the nineteenth century, when science was united with technology in the form of electrical and chemical works. Banking, investment, and monetary services grew apace. As Karl Marx had seen, the commercial market had become global.

A case can be made for a *sixth* period of globalization to be located in the nineteenth century, but I am not sure that it holds; rather it ought perhaps to be looked at simply as part of the fifth period. It is described by Joyce Chaplin as "the new globalisation of commodities . . . irreversible rearrangement of the natural world—a global reshuffling of plants, animals, people, and microbes . . . a redistribution of the world's material resources."[7] An example she cites is the breadfruit of the Pacific islands and the failed attempt by the British to turn it into a mere commodity, torn from its embedment in a cuisine—that is, "a whole cultural system."

The failure of the breadfruit, however, was not often duplicated; as we know, the commodification of produce and products implacably made its way across the world. In the end I think it better to include this entire development at the end of the nineteenth century as still part of a fifth period of globalization. This accords with the work of some economic historians who believe that the phenomenal extension of banking investment and manufacturing worldwide at this time justifies us in calling into question the assertions of a sixth period of globalization.

I believe that the case is otherwise. In my view a rupture occurs after World War II. With the coming of computers and satellites an extraordinary compression of time and space takes place. MNCs and NGOs are most evident in taking advantage of this instantaneous linkage. Moreover, each computer user is linked to every other one, in real time. We are all global.

What is more, we are conscious of our globalized condition. To capture the essence of the last three hundred years or so of the European past, historians have used the label *modernity*. Oddly, it is a term almost utterly unknown to the average layperson. In contrast, *globalization* is today on everybody's tongue. With the age of modernity giving way to the age of globalization, people are now conscious of the period in which they are living and writing and are aware of the process of which they are part.

It is in this present *sixth* period of globalization that historiography must also reorient itself. The nation-state no longer has the leading role on the world stage, though it still has a powerful secondary one. National archives are no longer the central source for our inquiries. Attention must now be paid more fully to MNCs and NGOs, to all sorts of international agencies and tribunals, and to global movements of all sorts. Our categories of thought must be readjusted.

A challenge to periodizing globalization should be noted before coming to a conclusion. It is the claim that it is postmodernity that should be seen as succeeding modernity. For a short time a popular mode of thought, postmodernity has now faded to a large extent because of its ideological baggage, but mainly because it defined itself in negative terms—that is, against modernity. It has held little explanatory power to describe the globalization that has been occurring after World War II.

Summarizing, we have been making the case that periodizing globalization is a warranted and heuristic action. The resulting classification sets up six periods: a first, characterized by hunter-gathers wandering over the globe; a second, marked by the so-called axial revolution of around fifth-century BC; a third, that of the fourteenth to sixteenth centuries, coincident with the European Renaissance; a fourth, distinguished by the world-encompassing ideas of the scientific revolution; a fifth, spun into existence by the Industrial Revolution; a sixth, revolving around the rupture caused by post–World War II globalization.

Can we discern in our periodizing of globalization any patterns? Has the time elapsed between one period and the next become shorter each time in a sort of Moore's law of globalization? Have technical inventions, such as printing, radio, and Internet played key roles, served as turning points, in the intensity and scope of interconnectedness? Has the intensity of increasing interdependence and interconnectivity become greater each time? Has the consciousness concerning the globalization process intensified and expanded? Differentially and in different parts of the world?

Can Norbert Elias's seminal work on the civilizing process be usefully applied in regard to globalization? As he argued, violence brought larger and larger social and political units into existence, and these units enforced peace and civility among their population. Will the final unity be that of a globalized humanity? If so, would this be the result of a cataclysmic conflict threatening to end all of civilization? Or can international institutions and mechanisms be established to bring about this final unity, a globalized humanity? Or is Elias's work, significant as it is, a throwback to nineteenth-century historiography, which saw history as a story of advancing civilization, a Western achievement—one that could be useful in the exercise of imperialism, with the white man reluctantly taking up his burden?

We end with a last question: Will further continuation of the process of globalization require further periodization—say, a seventh period? And what might be the technical innovation helping to bring it about? Will the process itself falter and become static or even regressive? Or will even a new rupture take place? The crystal ball is cloudy. All we know is that Finley's dictum about the nature of history and its need for classifications and divisions will remain operative. In that sense there is no rupture with the past.

## Notes

1.  M. I. Finley, *The Use and Abuse of History* (Penguin Books, 1987), 15.

2.  Martin Albrow, "Hiroshima: The First Global Event?" Paper presented to the Workshop on "Collective Memory and Collective Knowledge in a Global Age" at the Centre for the Study of Global Governance, London School of Economics and Political Science, April 17/18, 2007.

3.  Helge Jordheim, "Against Periodization: Koselleck's Theory of Multiple Temporalities," *History and Theory*, 51 (Mai 2012), 170.

4.  Johan Goudsblom, Eric Jones, and Stephen Mennell, *The Course of Human History: Economic Growth, Social Process and Civilization* (M.E. Sharpe, 1996).

5.  A. G. Hopkins (ed.), *Global History: Interactions between the Universal and the Local* (Palgrave Macmillan, 2006), 3.

6.  Jerry Bentley, "Cross-Cultural Interaction and Periodization in World History," *American Historical Review* vol. 101 (3), June 1996, p.757. The quotes that follow are on pages 758-9, 760, 763, 766, and 769.

7.  Joyce E. Chaplin, "What would the Tahitians say?" *London Review of Books*, May 24, 2012, 30-31.

# 7

# Global Importance of 1989

In 1789 the Bastille fell; 1989 marked the fall of the Berlin Wall. These two events, separated by two hundred years, both had momentous effects beyond their immediate impact on France and Germany. The French Revolution, of which the Bastille served as an opening salvo in what became a violent, continuing movement, reverberated throughout Europe up to Russia, and beyond in areas such as Turkey, Egypt, and the Americas. It was, in this sense, worldwide. The fall of the Berlin Wall, and the subsequent collapse of the Soviet Union and its empire, took place in a time and space that had become global. It was a nonviolent revolution, but its importance was even greater for all that. It, and the comparable events around it, just as with the 1789 event, can be thought of as a turning point or watershed.

Before proceeding to the actual events of 1989, we need to examine more carefully the historiographical questions surrounding the phrases just cited, which focus not on the continuities but on the presumed breaks in the human past. I will do so by instancing two names: the Dutch historian Jan Romein and the British historian Geoffrey Barraclough.

Romein is now almost completely forgotten. His mentor Johan Huizinga and his contemporary Pieter Geyl, especially the first, have had more enduring fame. Romein, who died in 1962, was a maverick historian, emphasizing that the past was not steady but marked by a series of lurches. He believed that if history were regarded in an integral fashion this fact would be obvious. His volume *The Watershed of Two Eras: Europe in 1900* (left in unfinished shape at his death, but completed by his widow from his papers), maintained that capitalism, led by Britain in its imperialist phase, was at its apex in 1900 but already losing its power to countervailing tendencies. This manifested itself in field after field—political, economic, cultural, etc.—whose combined results eventuated in Europe, and thus the world, entering a new period.

Romein was a Marxist, and one seems to hear the overtones of the notion of internal contradictions in his argument. But the Dutch historian was not an economic determinist, and his construction of the watershed is multicausal in nature. The English version of his book is over seven hundred pages, and we will not go into the details here. Much given to theoretical history, Romein's work is germane here mainly because of his argument emphasizing periodization, with a stress on the "turn of the last century." As he pointed out, between 1890 and 1914, we witness "the transformation of the traditional forms of domination into those of modern imperialism; the development of classical capitalism into a new type of banking and monopoly capitalism; the great landslide in which the masses for the first time joined the nations to play an active role in world developments."[1]

Ought we to see 1989 in similar watershed terms? Before deciding, let us also look at Geoffrey Barraclough, especially his *Introduction to Contemporary History* (1964). He also uses the image of "a watershed between two ages" when describing the years between 1890 and 1961.[2] More significantly, however, in dealing with a distinction he sees between "modern" and "contemporary" history, he resorts to the image of "turning points." These are marked by fundamental changes in the underlying structural features of the time. Even more clearly than his Dutch contemporary, Barraclough emphasizes that this is the perspective necessary to understand history, where "At every great turning-point of the past we are confronted by the fortuitous and the unforeseen, the new, the dynamic and the revolutionary."

Starting from a sense of living in a new period, the Englishman justifies the practice of contemporary history (breaking thereby with the previous domination of modern history), and foreshadows what we have come to call global and new global history.[3] Foregoing further details here, though noting the coincidence of the Dutchman and the Englishman both writing about the need for new periodization at the same time, again we turn to the question of whether watershed and turning point is the correct or most useful frame for our looking at 1989.

A vindication of this frame has already been prefigured in the volume *1956. European and Global Perspectives*.[4] Implicit in the conception of that book, this vindication is extrapolated and made explicit in the chapter by William R. Keylor when he remarks that "One is accustomed to regard the 1960s as the decisive decade of revolutionary transformations in many countries until the next great turning point in 1989-91."[5] Yet, even when so vindicated, the question remains: cannot every year be seen as a turning point of some sort, if connections are pursued forcefully enough? How about if one restricts oneself to a specific area, say, the arts or natural science?

Historians certainly seem to see many turning points in the past. Indeed, in a recent book edited by Byron Hollinshead and Theodore K. Rabb we are told on its cover that in it "Twenty Superb Historians Invoke Dramatic Turning Points in the History of Europe and the West."[6] And this is just in regard to Europe! Do we seem to be teetering on the edge of trivializing the idea?

It is clear that not all turning points are equal. To avoid the relatively trivial and hyperbolic use of the idea, we must focus on profound structural changes. Often, of course, these are not attached to a single date, but manifest themselves over the longue durée and only gradually. In regard to contemporary history, we come back to Geoffrey Barraclough and Jan Romein as our guides. Can we make the case that 1989 is such a profound example? Rather than trying to answer this query in the abstract, though remaining inspired by the general concept, let us turn to the events of 1989 themselves.

## (2)

The evidence suggests that in 1989 a concatenation of global events took place that altered the fundamental structures of contemporary human life and polity. They arise from a world turned global as a result of various globalization processes, and that these further extend these processes themselves. On the most global level, it is a question of various factors arising at the end of World War II that are best thought of as making for a rupture or break in historical periodization. We must talk now of a global epoch, and of a postmodern period, best addressed in my view in terms of what can be called new global history. On a slightly less universal level, we see that it is in this context that 1989 and its happenings can be viewed as punctuation points—turning points—in a globalized world.

Globalization, of course, does not occur overnight and once and for all. It has deep and extended roots in the past, gives rise to antiglobalization movements, and is not a deterministic matter. Marked as it is by increased interconnection and interdependency, it is unpredictable in its manifestations, and characterized by its contingent nature and way of unfolding. Moreover, we must constantly remind ourselves that globalization is always local, at the same time that the local takes on increasing global importance.

The fall of the Berlin Wall is the first of the epochal events that I want to address. As it happens, for me it started as a local experience. I was in Hungary for an economic conference at Lake Balaton that my wife was attending. On a particular day, the ninth of November 1989, our friend Andras Biro, an anthropologist, had invited us to visit his mother in a small village. As we approached, we saw a number of cars lining the street. Something was going on. One or two cars, Biro remarked, was understandable, for East Germans occasionally slipped over the border to buy produce, but this number was incredible. In fact, that day marked the fall of the wall, and East Germans were pouring over the border! So I experienced locally, as both the East Germans and Hungarians were doing at the same time, an historical event that was to have a global effect.

I must add that fate was conspiring for me in a special way. A year earlier, I had participated in a seminar at Boston University on global issues. Most of the other participants had been economists, or political scientists, or policy makers. I was the only historian. Back home, I began to think, what if one were to look at globalization in an historical perspective. Pursuing this line of thought I began to speculate on the concept of global history, talked to a few colleagues and ended up with a proposal for foundation support for an international conference to think about conceptualizing the subject. Thus, in 1989 my mind was filled with the general idea, and it was in terms of this context that the fall of the Berlin Wall took on significance for me.[7]

Needless to say, the event was first and foremost a German affair. It quickly took on regional—European—importance. On a more global scale, it marked the beginning of the end of the Cold War. This was a conflict that can be dated from 1947, when the Soviet Union began to interfere with traffic in Berlin. As Tony Judt remarked, "The real Cold War in Europe had begun."[8] Of course, as the Cold War continued it took on additional importance as shaping the appearance and tergiversations that characterized the Third World. In fact, as Odd Arne Westad has argued, its major importance should be estimated in non-European terms—in other words, as viewed globally, a view supported by the dying out with the end of the Cold War of the very concept of the Third World.[9] Indeed, the local had become global with a vengeance.

Let us return to the more local, the original place where history pivoted: the Berlin Wall. The wall, more concrete than the Iron Curtain in cutting off East Germany from the allure of the West, symbolized the division of Germany into two parts. That division, once the wall had fallen, was ended in 1990 by unification. This ending of the earlier split was made possible only by the fact that Gorbachev was in power in Moscow, where, as head of the Communist Party, he had introduced his policies of glasnost and perestroika. In the Soviet Union, he had been trying to accommodate his empire to the globalization taking place around it. In 1989, one result was that the fall of the Berlin Wall was allowed. Two years later, in 1991, the turn of the Soviet Union itself occurred; symbolized by Boris Yeltsin on top of a tank, the Communist regime and its empire collapsed from within.

Thus, we have noted a most momentous event, a true turning point. None of what I am recording is novel, but by placing these matters in a larger context, an integral history, we see them from a global perspective. Communism, in power in Russia for seventy years, and at the same time emerging as a superpower in the world at large, one of the two forces affecting the Third World during the time of the Cold War, simply ebbed away as a determining factor. This, surely, may be accounted a structural shift of epochal importance.

Like the proverbial stone thrown into the water, the fall of the Soviet Union had continuing ripples everywhere. Its East European satrapies were drastically affected. Many of them occupied an agricultural niche in the Soviet system, with whatever factories existed serving the military needs of mother Russia. All this now changed, as countries such as Moldova or Slovakia began turning to the West. As we all know, slowly and gradually they became candidates for the European Union. Thus, a geopolitical shift in the tectonics of Europe was grinding its way to a new structure built of political, economic, and cultural materials.

One could go on and on about the details of this shift, and social scientists have indeed undertaken this task with much distinction. Part of the novelty of 1989 was the rapidity with which events took place. Aided by the communications and media characteristics of globalization, often using the cover of environmental concerns, another aspect of the globalization process, the events were simply not predicted by the social scientists at the time. Surprise, therefore, is a dominant feature of our turning point.

(3)

The Soviet Union, of course, before its demise was only one part of the international Communist movement. The other was the huge landmass on its eastern border: the Chinese Communist state and society. It is in 1989 that state and society in China can be said to have clashed at Tiananmen Square. Then and there the massacres of June 4 occurred, making clear the nature of the Communist Party regime after Mao's death. The Party under Deng Xiaoping had already embraced market economics, thus taking the capitalist road.

The issue at Tiananmen Square was whether democracy would also be permitted.

The answer was symbolized by the dramatic picture of a young man in front of a tank, preventing it from going forward. In the end, of course, it did, and the democracy movement was crushed, figuratively as well as literally. China's extraordinary march to power and prosperity went forward meanwhile at a pace scheduled to bring it to parity with the United States, for example, by the middle of the twenty-first century. Whereas Russia's Communism was swept aside shortly after 1989; that of China has persisted in tandem with capitalism at least until now. Thus, a deep structural change took place in the Communist world, but in a particularly Chinese manner.

The entire international arena was reshaped by 1989 and its immediate consequences. As we noted, the Cold War was over. The Third World, freed from its shadow, now underwent a metamorphosis into what became known as the developing world, with China at first part of it and then on the way to becoming a superpower of sorts. The Soviet Union and its empire broke apart into the Russian Republic and its near neighbors in Eastern Europe, with both entities embracing some form of a market economy. China remained intact, both as to its holdings and its communist regime, regaining Hong Kong and retaining, for example, Tibet. Inasmuch as Communism remained a force in the world, its face henceforth appeared to be Chinese.

Two iconic images symbolize the course of events. The young man and the tank in Tiananmen Square embodies the Chinese development. The other shows Boris Yeltsin in 1991, on top of a Russian tank outside the Parliament building, as he led the move to put down the right-wing coup attempt versus Gorbachev. As the latter's protégé he saved his mentor, only to take his place a few years later. Subsequently, under Yeltsin's leadership, both capitalism and democracy were attempted in Russia. The former, as we know, flourished, persisting under his successor, Putin, while the effort at democracy has given way increasingly to an authoritarian regime.

Both the Russian and the Chinese developments were obviously rooted in the events of 1989. In the case of the fall of the Berlin Wall, it led shortly thereafter to the unification of Germany. It also influenced the dissolution of Russian unity and the end of its version of Communism. In the same momentous year, 1989, Tiananmen Square dramatically spotlighted the direction in which China was going: toward startling economic growth, in capitalist form, yet with the persistence of the Communist Party's authoritarian guidance and its opposition to formal democratization. As a turning point in contemporary history, 1989 indicates both roads taken and those not taken. What is striking is how interconnected the results of the turning point turn out to be.

## (4)

A decade before 1989, an Iranian ayatollah sat in France, sending cassettes and speaking by cell phone—quintessential devices of the contemporary globalization process—to his supporters in Tehran. The result in 1979 was the overturn of the American-backed regime of the Shah and the making of an Iranian Revolution. The background for this development was the intersection of Western imperialism and nationalism in Iran that led to the takeover of the oil fields by forces spearheaded by the left-wing nationalist Mossadec. Caught up in the Cold War, his government came to an end in August 1953 in a coup masterminded by the British and American intelligence agencies (specifically the CIA). At this point, the Shah's version of nationalism came into existence.

When the forces of the Ayatollah Khomeini overthrew the shah it also substituted for the latter's pro-American nationalism what was at first, as I have remarked, an Iranian national revolution.[10] This quickly turned, however, into an Islamic revolution whose nature was global. This rise of Islam must be situated in the events of 1978–9. These, in turn, were part of the Cold War, with the Soviet forces drawn into Afghanistan in 1980 by the need to support the local Communist party. In opposition, the United States and various Muslim countries began to support the mujahideen, the local Afghani freedom fighters, supplying them with stingers and other weapons versus airplanes and tanks (the ubiquitous tanks!). By February 15, 1989, the last Russian tank rumbled out of Afghanistan; the rule of Naijbullah, the Soviet figurehead left behind, lasted until his bloody death a few years later. Once again, as we note, the magic year 1989 appears in our account.

The rest, as we say, is history. The United States as Dr. Frankenstein had helped create a monster that took on global form in Al Qaeda. Using the tools of the communications revolution, a fundamentalist and radical Islam group transcended all borders, operating as if a multinational corporation, and with terrorism as its main weapon struck in numerous spots around the globe.[11] Aided by the misadvised invasion of Iraq, Al Qaeda found a fertile recruiting ground there as well as in the Israeli-Palestinian conflict, Pakistan, and the authoritarian regimes such as Egypt and even Saudi Arabia, from whence the charismatic leader Osama bin Laden had emerged. Pre-1989, the identified threat to Western-style capitalism and democracy had been Communism; now it was the terrorist version of Islam.

The Cold War had been mainly between two superpowers. Now the conflict was between the American superpower, and its allies, and an amorphous non-state actor. Outwardly religious in nature, radical Islam in fact was highly political. Above all, it transcended the usual territorial boundaries of nationalism, and although still fueled by a sense of national humiliation, fundamentally it had taken on a global shape and mission. We have seemingly come a long way from the events of 1989.

## (5)

Yet if we place all that we have said in the frame of turning points, we can see that we are dealing with structural changes of a profound nature, emanating from the events of that year. We have touched on such events as the fall of the Berlin Wall; the subsequent demise of the Soviet Empire and the end of Communism as a major contender for leadership of the world, marked by the withdrawal from Afghanistan of all Russian forces; the affair at Tiananmen Square, where China showed that it was the alternative leader of Communism but in a capitalist form that excluded democratic practice.

In another part of the world, we focused on the developments in the Middle East that saw the conflict of Western imperialism and nationalism in Iran, with the initial victory of the latter in 1979 and the return of the Ayatollah Khomeini to Tehran. Within months, that nationalist revolution had been turned into an Islamic one that is still coursing powerfully through the world. It is a world that is increasingly globalized, perhaps this being the most important and fundamental structural change of our epoch.[12]

As is obvious, I have not gone into much detail about any of the events of 1989—just enough to indicate their outlines. Nor have I dealt with other events of that year, such as the end of apartheid in South Africa, or the important turn taken by Japan at that time. For example, in regard to the latter, John Dower writes that "Hirohito's death in 1989 signaled the literal end of an era, the Showa period was over": Japan was witnessing "the true end of an epoch."[13] Instead of extending my list in this fashion, I have tried to place a limited but sufficient number of events in juxtaposition to one another, connected as they are by their eruption in 1989.

The definition of globalization is a contested one, as well it should be. But almost all such definitions include the fact of increased interconnection and interdependence. The global epoch humanity has recently entered into has its origin in the postwar period, and can be dated from the 1950s, 1960s, and every decade since. It is in this context that I have sought to place the happenings of 1989, as marking a turning point in that larger revolution of the historical world. In turn, those events must equally be viewed as causes of the increased globalization of our time. Depending on which end of the kaleidoscope one looks through, 1989 can be seen as a global happening with local manifestations or as a concatenation of local events with global importance.

## Notes

1.    Jan Romein, *The Watershed of Two Eras. Europe in 1900*, tr. Arnold J. Pomerans (Wesleyan University Press, 1978), xxx.

2.    Geoffrey Barraclough, *An Introduction to Contemporary History* (London: C.A. Watts & Co. LTD., 1964), 2. The next quote is from p. 3.

3.    For further treatment of Barraclough in these terms, see my article *Revisiting Barraclough's Contemporary History* in *Historically Speaking* (Vol. 8 (6), July 2007, 45–47) and an expanded version in the electronic journal *New Global Studies* (Vol. 2 (3), October 2008).

4.    Carole Fink, Frank Hadler, and Thomas Schramm (Eds.), *1956. European and Global Perspectives* (Leipziger Universitätsverlag, 2006).

5.    Ibid., 235–244.

6.    Byron Hollinshead and Theodore K. Raab, *I Wish I'd Been There: European History* (Doubleday, 2008).

7.    The conference took place at Bellagio in 1991 and gave rise to a book, *Conceptualizing Global History*, edited by myself and Ralph Buultjens (Boulder, CO.: Westview Press, 2003), the first in a

series, and a foundation stone for subsequent work in the new global history initiative, under the umbrella of the Toynbee Prize Foundation. The adjective "new" was subsequently added to "global history" in order to differentiate research and theorizing in this regard focused on the period after 1945, though still rooted in earlier times.

8.    Tony Judt, *Postwar Europe* (New York: Penguin Books, 2005), 126. In fact, Judt pushes the Cold War back a good ways, seeing it as starting at the end of World War I (103).

9.    Odd Arne Westad, *The Global Cold War* (New York: Cambridge University Press, 2007).

10.   For more on this substitution and the reasons for it, see "The Hidden Khomeini" in my book *The Leader, the Led, and the Psyche* (Hanover: Wesleyan Press, 1990).

11.   See further, for example, Olivier Roy, *Globalized Islam* (London: Hurst, 2004).

12.   Even in regard to globalization itself, the notion of turning point has already arisen. Thus, Harold James starts his talk on "The Future of Globalization: A Transatlantic Perspective" with the question, "Are we at a turning point in the development of globalization? Is the twenty-first century going to be very different from the late twentieth-century?" (A talk given to the Foreign Policy Research Institute on June 6, 2008). He casts his answer, it appears, in terms mainly and narrowly of economics and the end of the free market and the reaching of the limits of deregulation.

13.   John W. Dower, *Embracing Defeat: Japan in the Wake of World War II* (New York: W.W. Norton and Co., 1999), 558. A page later, he says that "Nineteen forty-five was unquestionably a watershed year—as momentous as 1868, when the feudal regime was overthrown and the new Meiji government established." Dominic Sachsenmaier underlined for me the importance of what was happening in 1989 in Japan.

# 8

# Globalization Nationalized

For many social scientists, globalization is eroding the forces of nationalism. The latter is frequently seen as a consequence of modernity, with the processes of globalization, especially during the last half century, now replacing modernity and its resultant nationalism. The literature on this subject has been growing, and is important. I myself have contributed to it in various places. It is not that aspect of the subject, however, to which I am devoting my attention here.

Rather, I wish to examine the way in which nationalism, in subtle and obvious ways, seeks to use globalization for its own purposes. It is a kind of "if you can't beat them, join them," although, in fact, it is a way of beating them by other means.

Now it is true that in the nineteenth century, voices were raised seeking to enlist national feeling in the course of a wider adherence to humanity. Thus the Italian patriot Giuseppe Mazzini spoke glowingly of his commitment to Italian nationalism and the emerging nation-state that it animated as part of his larger adherence to mankind. In this he was echoing the words of Goethe, extolling a cosmopolitan ethos, declaring that the aim of national feeling was "not uniformity . . . but mutual understanding and tolerance between nations through the revelation of universal humanity."[1] This reminder that nationalism can be seen as a form of social binding, not incompatible with larger ties, is important as we proceed with our inquiry.

With that said, let us look at some of what is happening as national aims wrap themselves in a seeming embrace of the global. A recent conference—Global History, Globally—illustrates this point exceptionally well.[2] Papers on Korea, Turkey, Australia, China, the UK, Japan, and others show quite specifically how the appropriation of the global for national purposes is carried out. In an especially brilliant account of historiographic developments in Korea, Jie-Hyun Lim argues persuasively that "various orientations of transnational history, once presumed as the alternative to competing national histories in East Asia, accommodated and even served nationalist agenda."[3]

The road leading to this development is itself transnational. It is Japan that mirrors the rise of European national histories, and in this mirror both pursues and narrates its own path to national history in the nineteenth and twentieth centuries. As Jie-Hyun Lim then informs us, Korean national history was "a product of a similar attempt, except with Japan in the place of 'West.'" Thus, there is a "global chain of national histories."[4] It is a subtle and complicated argument, in which transnationalism first serves the course of Japanese and Korean national histories, and then transmutes itself into global history while still serving the cause of national history.

It should not surprise us that as globalization brings East Asian countries into closer relations, it also heightens national tensions. Indeed, this is true in regard to globalization all over the world and in regard to all polities. As nations are tied more closely to one another, such connections give rise to increased tension and a pull to difference and particularism. This is the constant tug of war between universalism and the local and relative. The examples of Japan and Korea bear out this generalization, where specifics can be found. It is in this context, and within varying local contexts, that transnational and now global history is subject to national appropriation.

My next example is the People's Republic of China. Repeatedly humiliated by Western and other powers in the nineteenth century, China turned to nationalism with Sun Yat-Sen and later Chiang Kai-Shek, then Communism with Mao Tse-tung, and capitalism with Deng Xiaoping, while retaining socialist features and a Communist Party control apparatus. Into this mixed bag of ties holding the country together, efforts were also made to revive Confucian teachings and ideals and other traditional elements of China's heritage.[5] It is into this mix, now occurring in a time of increased globalization, that the theme of nationalism persisted or was reawakened.

My personal entry into this problem occurred via an e-mail message from China. It informed me of the existence of a new journal and asked if I would contribute something. The journal, published in Beijing, was called *Chinese Global History Review*, and it was primarily concerned with world and global history, to which I added new global history (i.e., post–World War II globalization). My assignment was to write on all three fields or approaches.

The interest of Chinese historians in these subjects was obviously rooted in a desire to share in the efforts to escape Eurocentrism found in the West but mostly in the fact that China was now a significant player in the unfolding global processes. In my submission, I gave a good deal of attention to new global history, after comparing it to world and global history, and then commented that "Now globalization is seen as an enterprise being undertaken by the whole of the human species; and requiring the attention of all peoples."[6]

In this oblique manner I was suggesting to Chinese historians that, like Mazzini a century earlier, they needed to serve both nationalistic aims and those of a larger humanity.

There is much in the Chinese heritage that lends itself to this larger purpose; and, indeed, I am optimistic that China will sooner or later move in this direction. My editor at the new journal, however, was troubled by my message and demurred at its inclusion. Global history at the moment was too important as a supporter in the cause of nationalism to be enlisted also in a larger human cause. Subsequently I have seen neither the translation of my article nor heard any further news of the journal (nor can it presently be found on Google). A finger in the wind (and which wind?), this small incident was another item in my consideration of how globalization and its histories can be listed in the ranks of national history.

Support for my position comes from recognized scholars of China such as Q. Edward Wang. As he observes, after 1949, when the Communists took power in China, world history became a legitimate field in historical study, basing itself on the Marxist vision.[7] This was not the case with the nationalists who had retreated to Taiwan. As for the mainland Chinese world historians, one obvious desire was to compare their status with the advanced societies of the West. In fact, as Wang tells us, a "Research Center for Global History was established in 2004, headed by Liu Xincheng, a historian of early modern Europe who also recently became his university's president. Under the guidance of Liu and his colleagues, a dozen or so Chinese students are currently working on their master and doctoral degrees, hoping to become 'global historians.'" In these developments, we can also see the presence of national aspirations.

The new center is at Capital Normal University, and it is strongly connected to the *Journal of World History*, and its

capable editor Jerry Bentley. The *JWH* is a font of considerations on world history, with much attention to China and
its entry into the field. A typical recent article is Luo Xu,
"Reconstructing World History in the People's Republic
of China since the 1980s," which details the various barri-
ers to the effort "to envision a world history with Chinese
characteristics."[8] Other articles by Q. Edward Wang can
also be found there. Summing up much of this work, Wang
concludes that each attempt at global history also invariably
derives from and is circumscribed by a "localized concern
and even a nationalist interest."[9]

What if we turn from China to the United States? Here
we have both a flourishing discipline of history much concerned with world and global history and a country seen by
many as the epitome of an embrace of globalization. Looked
at more closely, however, we see that in this vein globalization is equated with the spread of the free market, American
style, and in favor of American interests. Until the financial
debacle of the recent months, this sort of globalization was
applauded in spite of its unevenness and its harmful aspects
as it impinged on many peoples and aspects of the economy.
While obviously the economic was and is one part of the contemporary globalization process, its uncritical embrace was
more ideological and reductionist than the result of careful
examination and judicious understanding. Such simplicity,
needless to say, served the purposes of American nationalism.
To look at globalization as a whole is to see that the political,
cultural, technological, and similar aspects of actual social
life surround the economic and qualify its simple-minded
free existence.[10]

Back in the 1940s and '50s, the role of the United States
in international affairs seemed also to foster the global
aspect. The nation was instrumental in the establishment of
the UN and its pursuit of the four freedoms, and especially

of the Universal Declaration of Human Rights, presaging a new era in substituting or supplementing human concerns for national sovereignty. However, this direction was quickly aborted when America began to realize that it could not control the agenda of the world community when its impulses went beyond America's national interests. Increasingly, as this became evident, the United States became hostile to the UN. This was shockingly obvious in the post-Reagan years when, with the Cold War finally over and the other nations of the world seeking to steer relatively independent courses, the rise of the Bush administration made its intentions clear in the new National Security Doctrine. As in the Iraq invasion, America would act unilaterally when necessary in the name of its interests.

These interests were no longer coincident with those of an emerging global civil society, but those of a highly nationalistic United States. With its idealistic veneer, expressing a thin strip of American reality, it is often overlooked exactly how nationalistic the country is. Poll after poll showing this fact is frequently ignored—America is one of the most nationalistic of peoples—and the abundant history underpinning its nationalist inclinations (partly hidden by the form of empire in which it exists) simply obscures the reality. And America's constant self-laudation as the benevolent and supportive leader in foreign aid and humanitarian efforts is dust in the eye of reality. Of course, there is a certain amount of reality; enough to obscure the fact that the United States, like Korea and China, has nationalist aims as it embraces various features of globalization.

Does such nationalism extend to its world and global historians? Interestingly, the conference on Global History, Globally did not have a paper devoted to the subject in the United States comparable to those on other parts of the globe, such as Korea, Japan, China, etc. To attempt such a study might require a conference similar in size to the one on GHG. An equally needed conference is one on American hypocrisy. It is not that other nations do not also speak and act in hypocritical terms; it is the American air of innocence. Over the decades we have not only baffled our friends but ourselves in the process.

World and global history promises to redeem some of this complacency. At its best moments, it does. But, as many critics have pointed out, practitioners of world history in America are still mostly Eurocentric. And global historians are often in the same boat. This tendency is abetted by methodological nationalism, or the fact that most archives and collections of statistics are organized along nation-state lines. Further, many still see, consciously or unconsciously, globalization as a form of Americanization. Needless to say, recent financial events have weakened this confidence. A closely aligned form, as noted, is to equate globalization with the free market; this, too, has been a badly shaken faith recently. A vacuum of belief has been created, which global historians can fill with a holistic approach, which demotes the economic factor from its position of primacy and partners it with the political, social, cultural, and so forth with which it always actually exists. Real historical analysis can and should take over from ideology.

With the nationalist inclinations of American historians practicing world history and global history admitted, it must be added that many do seek a transnational perspective that is truly such. It may be that such historians are further along the curve of realizing that to existing national ties and interests must increasingly be added those of humanity at large, partly because the United States plays such a major role in creating the global problems that cry out for global solutions: climate, energy, military, political all bear the large footprint of Uncle Sam. The historians engaged in the truly transnational are ahead of their government—out of sync?—but hopefully are pointing the way. Or it may be that intellectuals tend to be disregarded, or disparaged by the general US democracy and the powers that be. Or that the latter are satisfied by the unreflective nationalism of those who, like historians in Korea, Japan, and China, for example, write global history in a fashion that serves the nationalist agenda.

This last is a very natural development. In the last three centuries or so, the national ties became an important source of identity and connections for many people. It became the social bond par excellence, either in practice or theory. It offers additional support to links rooted in family, tribe, and regional bindings. Now global historians are recognizing the national interest is increasingly tied to the global. To be a good subject of the national polity means also being a good global subject. This realization is slowly creeping into the public perception, and is partly inspired by and reflected in the writings of global historians. To go further along this route, all world and global historians have to keep in mind the entity of humanity in their accounts.

To truly rise above the nationalist tendency, while paying it due accord, the historian needs to constantly add the perspective of humanity. What has been the effect on humanity of, say, the American purchase of Louisiana, as well as on the expansion of the original colonies? Of Andrew Jackson's Presidency? Of the British wars with Napoleon, not only in terms of the formation of the British Empire but the cause of humanity? Similar questions must be raised in all other histories: Chinese, Indian, and so forth. And these considerations must be taken into account systematically and constantly and not just occasionally and by indirection.

Elsewhere I have argued that via the notion of crimes against humanity, in the post–World War II period, the concept of Humanity emerged.[11] This has been the result of both globalization and a judicial revolution, culminating for the moment in the International Criminal Court. The concept's emergence is rooted in the earlier phases of globalization, but takes on body in the last half-century or so. Thus, there is a guide to help us as we look back over episodes in world history and global history accounts, seeking ways to avoid simply listing them unreflectively in the cause of national histories.

Even without such measures, a caution such as the present article may alert us to hidden dangers and put us on our guard as we pursue our work in world and global history. This holds for all time periods and all areas. I have instanced Korea, China, and the United States. The rest of the world and its histories can be added to this list. A world and global history true to itself can do no less.

## Notes

1.  *Daedalus*, vol. 137, (3), Summer 2008, back page.
2.  This conference, *Global History, Globally*, was convened at Harvard University on February 8–9, 2008, under the auspices of Sven Beckert and Dominic Sachsenmaier.
3.  Papers from *Global History, Globally*, unpublished conference proceedings, 7.
4.  Ditto, 3 and 4.
5.  Especially worth reading in this regard is Martin Jacques, *When China Rules the World* (2009) and Alan T. Wood, *All Under Heaven*, still in ms. Jacques's title is misleading; he is really considering China as part of a globalized world, not ruling it.
6.  Bruce Mazlish, unpublished.
7.  Jacques, op. cit., 16. The following quote, 19.
8.  *Journal of World History*, Sept. 2007, ii.
9.  *Global History, Globally*, op. cit., 28.
10. For a far better sort of economics, see Neva Goodwin et al. *Microeconomics in Context* (M. E. Sharpe, 2002), *Macroeconomics in Context* (M. E. Sharpe, 2002).
11. See Bruce Mazlish, *The Idea of Humanity in a Global Era* (Palgrave Macmillan, 2009).

# 9

# From the Sentiment of Humanity to the Concept of Humanity*

In eighteenth-century Western Europe, the phrase "sentiment(s) of humanity" was quite common. A classical locus was in the works of David Hume. Although he used the phrase in various ways, it seems most frequently to be employed in connection with the notion of sympathy. It is the notion of the sentiment of humanity connected to that of sympathy and the latter to benevolence that provides the nexus of meaning for the phrase. In this nexus, we find for Hume the components of morality.

Thus it was perceived by Hume's contemporaries. Writing to him in 1761, the Frenchwoman Hippolyte de Saujon congratulated him on his *History of England* and added that his work "fills the heart with sentiments of humanity and benevolence."[1] Later scholars, analyzing Hume's work, see his idea of humanity as "fundamentally dependent on sympathy."[2] Sympathy was one of the most prevalent words in the eighteenth through early nineteenth centuries.

Adam Smith, who admired Hume, wrote *The Theory of Moral Sentiments*, emphasizing that there was in each of us an "impartial spectator," who constantly asked, "What will my actions look like to others?" This, then, influenced our actual actions. The other influence on us was, of course, the sentiment of humanity. Smith equated this with benevolence. His treatment of the subject is not always consistent, and in one place his remarks invoke the gender question. Claiming that generosity is different from humanity, he states that "Humanity is the virtue of a woman, generosity of a man. The fair sex, who have commonly much more tenderness than ours, have seldom so much generosity. That women rarely make considerable donations, is a observation of the civil law. Humanity consists merely in the exquisite fellow-feeling which the spectator entertains with the sentiments of the persons principally concerned, so as to grieve for their sufferings. . . ."[3]

Needless to say, Smith is better known for the book *The Wealth of Nations*, in which he puts benevolence aside (though it is to be assumed as necessary for the system to function) and analyzes the workings of self-interest, in the process establishing the classical foundations for the science of economics. Yet, we must not forget that that work assumes the gyrations on the sentiment of humanity in which Smith had indulged.

What is clear from what has been said so far—and an entire book could be written on the subject—is that the sentiment of humanity was an ontological statement about human nature, and not an observation about the reality of Humanity and its being a possible source of sovereignty. One question arises at this point. Was the notion of a "sentiment of humanity" unique to Western culture, or to be found elsewhere as well?

I have tried to consult experts in both Chinese and Islamic studies on exactly this point. One broad-ranging scholar on China responded as follows: "I guess 'sentiment of humanity' could be rendered into 'renqing,' something like human emotions (it is human plus sentiment, emotions). The concept of humanity is a modern one, 'renlei,' which translates literally into something like 'humankind.' Anthropology, for instance, is translated as 'renlei xue,' study of renlei. I am not aware of any premodern native term that would be the equivalent of 'humanity' as concept, which did not exist."[4]

In regard to Islam, an eminent scholar responded to my query:
"The Koran uses different words to describe human beings as follows:

1.  Adam: in genealogical term
2.  Bashar: in physiological term
3.  Insan: in Aristotelian term: as opposed to animals

Otherwise, I don't think that Islam recognizes the concept of Humanity as we know it today. Islam uses the term UMMA, not Humanity."[5]

Are the roots of such a sentiment, if not a concept, of humanity to be found in the West in its classical period? There we appear to encounter a fateful union of Stoicism and early Christianity. As one scholar puts it, "both Stoicism and Christianity occupied some ground in common, and both adumbrated an all-inclusive order for a world citizenry. Each from its own premises sought to include all the peoples of the earth in a single community, a single humanity."[6]

In the fragmented feudal society of the European Middle Ages, the sentiment held little if any meaning (except, perhaps, among the Scholastics). Christianity, of course, prevailed, but its actions belied any pretense to a concern with the sentiment. Instead, sectarian wars in which Christians fought Christians were the reality, along with schisms and heresies, all to be dealt with in murderous fashion. By the time of the Renaissance, however, voices concerning themselves with humanity began to be heard. The famous example of

Bartolome de las Casas arguing that the Indians of the New World were humans (and therefore convertible to the true religion) is perhaps the most renowned.

As should be clear, I am not trying to write a history of the sentiment of humanity, but only to touch on some of its highlights. The Renaissance, with its rediscovery of the classical writers, and the New World discoveries making people aware of the extent of the globe and an awareness of different people on it, but all human, gave a vigorous fillip to the general idea. One who spoke eloquently in the light of these revelations was Michel de Montaigne, who used the phrase *commun humain*.

That Europe soon fell into the squabbles of the Reformation period is too well known to need much attention here. Both Catholics and Protestants dehumanized and sought to exterminate each other. Finally, exhausted by incessant civil war, both sides allowed a drift toward tolerance to take place. By the time of the Enlightenment, mainly in France but in all parts of Europe (in this case including England), the climate of opinion could be permeated by the sentiment of humanity.

The distinction between civilized and barbarian goes back at least to antiquity. The reified word civilization, however, dates only from 1756, when Victor Riqueti Mirabeau in his *L'Ami des hommes* first introduced the term. Within a decade the term was a commonplace throughout Europe. By the nineteenth century, it had become a device whereby Western imperialism imposed itself elsewhere. It is at this time, also, when the phrase "crimes against civilization and humanity" began to appear. It is only at the time of the Nuremberg Trials that the word civilization is dropped, and the charge against the Nazis and their horrors is phrased as crimes against humanity.

Now I want to move on to a different, though affiliated, idea: the concept of Humanity. The road to it is a long and twisting, and often surprising, one, with many branches not taken. In nineteenth-century Europe it is frequently coupled with the terms Christianity and or civilization. Surprising perhaps to some it is tsarist Russia that was in the lead. The great international legalist Sazonov was at its head.[7] A few Chinese scholars at the end of the century raised the issue in regard to race, claiming equality on the basis of a common humanity.

The idea of Humanity was still more in the clouds above the heads of philosophers than in the texts of legal jurists until the event of the Turkish handling of the Armenian Question. Were the terrible actions committed in the 1915 period a massacre or a case of genocide? This is still a hotly contested question. What is not in question is that under Ottoman rule over one million Armenians died in the operation aimed at expelling them from the Empire. As one account tells us, governments around the world announced "their intent to hold the Turks individually and collectively accountable for these gross violations of the most basic of all human rights—namely, the right to exist—and 'crimes against humanity.'"[8]

Ineffectual trials—the so-called Constantinople or Malta trials—were held, but amounted to almost nothing, then or now as a precedent. Only with World War II and the consequent Nuremberg Trials did memories briefly touch on the Constantinople example. It was the 1945 juridical proceedings that etched the phrase "crimes against humanity" on the human consciousness. Of course, the question immediately arises, what is this humanity that is sinned against? Indeed, this is the starting point for my own inquiry into the concept of Humanity.

It is requisite, I believe, to place the inquiry in the context of post–World War II globalization. Let us now turn directly to that subject. Globalization by now is a clearly acknowledged phenomenon. What exactly that phenomenon is, however, is a hotly debated question. The term itself achieves currency, it appears, sometime in the 1950s, and widespread usage by the 1970s. Its definition emphasizes that it means increased interconnectivity and interdependence among peoples and societies. Once the concept has been formed, it can then be extended retroactively to the past. Thus, globalization can be said to have been taking place from the time of the hunter-gatherers to the present. It is as if Moliere's *bourgeois gentilhomme* suddenly realized he has been speaking prose.

I want to argue that we gain a much greater understanding by looking at globalization as a rupture that opens up after World War II.[9] What are some of the factors that compose the process, or processes, of globalization, for we must make concrete and subject to further research what is involved?

During the War, rocketry was much developed. As recounted earlier, an earlier predecessor was the Russian scientist, Konstantin Tsiolkovsky who in 1903 published his exploration of the principles involved. On this basis came the artificial satellites (the moon is a natural one) that so distinguish our era. The first launch into space was the Russian Sputnik in 1957. This was an Earth-orbiting satellite, and triggered a space arms race between the Soviet Union and the United States.[10] Subsequently, hundreds and hundreds of satellites were launched by both superpowers, with thousands floating around as debris.

Along with these advancements in technology and the computer revolution came communication in instant time and space which facilitated the growth of multinational companies. Thus, whereas in 1969 their number was estimated at 7,258 they had soared to 63,000 in the year 2000. We are faced with a J-shaped curve.[11] This growth has inspired economists and economic historians to equate globalization tout court with economic, generally free market, development.

Clearly, the economic is a powerful factor in the growth of globalization. It is, however, not the only one. Indeed, the economic is never just the economic; it is always combined with the technological, political, social, and cultural.[12]

Moreover, the political implications of globalization, in an epoch of profound climate change and ecological exhaustion, have arisen, even when lacking in institutional solutions. The social implications, under which we should include migrations, are equally important. Under both social and cultural we should include the growth of NGOs. Although a detailed research project such as that of the MNCs has not (yet) been undertaken, we can assume that NGOs will show a similar J-shaped curve. As for the cultural, its globalized nature is obvious everywhere, especially in regard to the arts. Lastly and most importantly in my view is global consciousness, evident in the very coining of the term sometime in the 1950-60s, and its obtaining widespread currency in the 1970-80s. To my mind, this may be the most important feature of globalization. Humans and societies everywhere, though in a disparate manner, are coming to realize that we are all on one planet, and share global problems even in our most local concerns.[13]

As discussed before, the most profound result in my view is that globalization, combined with vital other elements, is producing and instituting Humanity that inhabits the ground and not the skies as envisioned by previous thinkers such as Kant. Long the preserve or vision of philosophers, it was during the Nuremberg trials of 1945-46 that legal judgment was brought to bear on crimes against humanity. A judicial revolution, as I have called it, began at that time.[14] First, along with war crimes, war itself was seen as a crime. This marks a true revolution in the course of humanity's history. Along with this shift came the charge of crimes against humanity and the question of what this humanity is that had been sinned against.

It is with this question that the development of the *concept* of Humanity can be said to have begun. The concept emerges over time and is a social construct that has more force in certain societies than in others. It gains power as it allows people everywhere an identity including, while transcending, that of their local, national, and religious ties. It gathers force from what the philosopher Ian Hacking has called "dynamic nominalism." Thus we are told that "once you invent a category—as, for example, the category of 'homosexual' seems to have been invented in the late nineteenth century—people will sort themselves into it, behave according to the description, and thus contrive new ways of being."[15]

People and societies are facilitated in recognizing their common Humanity by the computer revolution, which puts them in touch with another instantly, and by the globalization process that is playing out around them. Humanity is not just acted on, as in crimes against humanity, but becomes a sovereign force itself—and promises to be increasing so in the future.

It is useful at this point to look at two related topics, which are seen as having some sort of affinity with the concept of Humanity: humanitarianism and human rights. The former, not to be confused with development aid, according to recent research seems a case of "the road to hell is paved with good intentions." The donor, of course, feels virtuous. Such aid can also serve the giver's national interests. On the face of it, it seems cruel to criticize such well-intentioned efforts. It is only on closer inspection that it turns out that most of the aid ends up in the pockets of dictators. For details that make for a very persuasive case, I cite three sources in a footnote.[16] To add insult to injury, humanitarian aid is also accused of being a part of imperialist outreach. In any case, it appears to have little to do with the concept of Humanity.

This is not true of the subject of human rights. It is either directly connected or certainly so by affinity. Like so many other subjects it is both intellectually and politically contentious. Intellectually, there is debate over its origins. A number of scholars have argued for its beginnings in the West. Thus, the distinguished historian of Renaissance and Reformation history John Headley has extended his interest to the modern period and vigorously asserted that human rights (and political dissension) have their roots in the European tradition, from whence it spread to the rest of the globe. Another historian, Lynn Hunt, has investigated its emergence at the time of the Enlightenment and the French Revolution.[17]

Others see this view as Eurocentric. They find evidence of human rights thinking in other cultures, such as the Chinese. Naturally, there is much debate as to the meaning of human rights. One such right, stemming mainly from the decolonization experience, though with earlier assertions, is the right to self-determination. This, of course, reinforces national sovereignty, and often results in the peoples involved being terrorized by their own tyrants, who oppose human rights. John Stuart Mill argued that better government often emerged from foreign rule, for example, the British in India, than from the local leaders. He obviously underestimated the feelings of nationalism. In any case, with the right of self-determination the universality supposedly inhering in the idea disappears. There is also left hanging the question of how far down the ladder the right to self-determination should be honored.

It appears that the first use of the phrase *human rights* entered the English language in the 1940s.[18] This had no connection with the Nuremberg trials, which spored so much else. Also about this time, it became gender neutral, shifting from the rights of man to human rights. However, the idea did not enjoy widespread usage at the time. That shift had to wait until the 1970s, when human rights became a movement. It was in this new atmosphere that President Jimmy Carter could speak of human rights as a foreign policy goal of the United States. (Whether intended or not, the phrase became a centerpiece of the attack on the Soviet Union during the Cold War.) It was also in the '70s, in fact 1977, that the Nobel Peace Prize was awarded to Amnesty International, an outstanding NGO in the field.

Much discussion took place as to whether to put the emphasis on individual or communal rights, with the West generally on one side and Asia and Africa on the other. The communal argument was obviously closely linked to the idea of self-determination. Of special note is the final Helsinki Act of 1973-75, in which the Soviet Union unthinkingly allowed a Trojan Horse into their empire. Out of the Helsinki Watch, incidentally, came the Human Rights Watch, one of the major NGOs working in the area.

Recently, Columbia professor Samuel Moyn published a book, *The Last Utopia: Human Rights in History* (Harvard/ Belknap, 2010), whose title suggests his take on the subject. There is definitely a millennial note to the human rights harmony. I also agree with him that the Westphalian system of nation-states competing with one another is still abundantly around us. He underestimates, I believe, the power of the human rights movement, and its self-fulfilling nature, as well as its soft power aspect. Realists and Realpolitik generally underestimate the power of ideas and ideals. When Stalin rhetorically asked, "How many divisions does the pope have?" he thought the answer clear. One must pause, however, to remember that Stalin is no longer around, while the Papacy (in its own way as authoritarian as Stalin) still flourishes.

With some of the essential facts about human rights established, especially its existence as idea and as movement, we can now turn to its connection with globalization and the concept of Humanity. The former, the process of globalization, appears to facilitate greatly the movement itself. It makes it easier for people to see that they are not alone. With that sense comes a feeling of empowerment. Repressive governments, aware of this fact, seek to clamp down on the computers that connect people and can mobilize thousands in instantaneous time. The Jasmine Revolutions of 2011 in the Middle East make this clear.

The relation of human rights and the concept of Humanity is more complicated. To begin with, let us note that for many people, the use of the term humanity is a form of imperialism. It can be used, and has been, to justify foreign intervention in a number of cases. To paraphrase a famous statement, "When I hear the word humanity, I reach for my gun." There is little question but that the name humanity has been evoked in contexts that are hardly praiseworthy. This pejorative usage, however, should not prevent a better use. The word democracy, for example, has been grievously misused in numerous cases. Yet one would not want to abandon its use in a proper fashion.

The opposite of Humanity is dehumanization. If one can dehumanize one's opponent, see him as just an animal—vermin—then one need not have any compunction in exterminating that individual or group. It is not just the Nazis who followed this path, but many others, including, for example, American colonists in regard to the Native Americans. In a perverse way, dehumanization can be seen as the flattery paid by its perpetrators to virtue.

Human rights are by definition to apply to Humanity everywhere. It is a universal attribute. This is denied in many parts of the world, in the name of national sovereignty and cultural relativity. The battle is joined between the forces of national sovereignty and the transcending claims of Humanity. It is played out in the international judicial arena, with many states, including the United States, unwilling to submit to external judgment. Thus, the battle for Humanity must necessarily be played out on the fields of the nation. A country such as China claims exemption from human rights claims (seen as a Western intrusion), and thus implies that it is outside Humanity. There are many others in its company.

It is against these walls—in the case of China a new Great Wall—that the battering ram of Humanity must exert itself. It is not intended to destroy local cultures, but to add an additional layer to them. It cherishes the local culture as an essential contributor to Humanity, which celebrates diversity under its wings.

## (2)

The subject of human rights exists in close affinity to the sentiment of humanity and its transition to the concept of Humanity. There are two ways of approaching the subject, one historical and the other more philosophical. Both are informative. The historical route seems fairly straightforward. Building on natural law, it would seem to have burst forward in its own right at the time of the American and French Revolutions. The American Declaration of 1776 in its second paragraph begins, "We hold these truths to be self-evident, that all men are created equal, that they are endowed by their Creator with certain unalienable Rights, that among these are Life, Liberty and the pursuit of Happiness." Then follows a list of specific wrongs done to his people by the British king, George III. This specificity is often forgotten.

The French Declaration of the Rights of Man (and Citizen, as it is usually referred to) is filled with resounding generalizations. In seventeen short articles we are told about the "natural, unalienable, and sacred rights of man." These rights are "liberty, property, security, and resistance to oppression." Other details follow. Critics have pointed out ever since the defects and limitations of both the American and French declarations. In the American case, all men are created equal—except presumably blacks. In the French case, women are not included as equals. In an impassioned tome, Mary Wollstonecraft pointed out the iniquity in her *Vindication of the Rights of Women* (1792). Nevertheless, with all their defects, both declarations set out noble aims, to be realized over time and with much struggle.

Do we encounter comparable statements at the time about the sentiment of humanity and the line connecting it to human rights in any other society or culture, in any other part of the world than the West? The answer seems to be no. Gradually in the nineteenth century, with the rise of an international system based on the achievement of civilization, the idea of human rights seems to spread. Indeed, by the twentieth century, human rights (especially in regard to religion) has become a stick with which to beat non-European countries and to justify intervention. Hypocrisy is to be found everywhere.

No wonder the others were resistant to its acceptance. Human rights was a foreign notion, imposed often at the end of a gun. Let us call a spade a spade: human rights was and is a Western innovation (would that we could also refer to a Chinese spade and an Islamic one). Its claim to be universal, like a law of physics, was met with derision by its victims. They proffer, instead, an argument in terms of cultural relativism.

This seems to be the current situation. Now let us regard it philosophically. Cultures and societies are not impervious monoliths. They are constantly awash with borrowings, voluntarily or imposed (of course, this can make a difference). From the Islamic world came Arabic numerals and the concept of zero, replacing the unwieldy Roman ones. In the twelfth century, there also came from the Arab region the recovered classics of Greek and Latin antiquity. Gunpowder and the compass came to Europe around the fourteenth century from China.

We should also note that by the twenty-first century the entire notion of East and West had become an anachronism. Seen from space, there is no such meaningful perspective. One need only look at a book such as *The Myth of Continents*[19] to secure an idea of the implications of such changed vision. Global space is different from previous optics.

In this perspective, it no longer makes sense to speak of East and West. The world has become one, encompassed, even if to varying degrees, by the processes of globalization. Assimilation in terms of a science and technology must be accompanied by a similar assimilation in terms of a social universal, that of Humanity. So many of our major problems are global in compass, such as climate change and ecological exhaustion (a water crisis looms just ahead) that they can only be dealt with in a global manner. The over three-hundred-year reign of the Westphalian system, with the nation-state at its core, is now increasingly an anachronism.

Its demise or rather its sinking into senescence will not be without much pain and conflict, even unto a state of crisis. Such a state of crisis, to paraphrase Dr. Johnson's remark about the sight of the guillotine concentrating one's mind, is both an opportunity and a possible precipice. It will be our choice whether we act like lemmings or bring about a new world and a newly conceived Humanity, assimilating innovations and contributions made from all over the globe.

## Notes

\* A version of this chapter first appeared in *Historically Speaking*, vol. XIII (3), (June 2012).

1.    *The New York Times*, 5/7/11, A9.

2.    Remy Debes, "Humanity, Sympathy and the Puzzle of Hume's Second Enquiry," *British Journal for the History of Philosophy* 15 (1), 2007: 28. Further on sympathy, see Bruce Mazlish, *A New Science*. The Breakdown of Connections and the Birth of

Sociology (Oxford, 1989; paperback, University of Pennsylvania Press, 1993), 15-18 and passim.

3.    Adam Smith, *The Theory of Moral Sentiments* (Oxford University Press, 1976), 190-191.

4.    Arif Dirlik, e-mail May 12, 2011, in response to my query. I am grateful for his help in this matter.

5.    E-mail, May 11, 2011, from Mehdi Mozaffari. He then adds that "some Muslim poets and thinkers have expressed their feeling for Humanity elegantly."

6.    John Headley, "Global History and the West's Universalizing Process," unpub. ms., 3.

7.    See the paper "The Origins of 'Crimes against Humanity': The Russian Empire, International Law, and the 1915 Note on the Armenian Genocide," presented to the Harvard International and Global History Seminar at Harvard University, February 24, 2010. This is a pathbreaking and stimulating paper.

8.    Paul Gordon Lauren, *The Evolution of International Human Rights* (University of Pennsylvania Press, 1980), 87. This is a most comprehensive treatment of its subject. Especially focused on the Armenian issue per se is Taner Akcam, *A Shameful Act. The Armenian Genocide and the Question of Turkish Responsibility* (Holt, 2006).

9.    Historians, although mostly seeing the past as a continuum, also need rubrics under which to indicate breaks. For a discussion of this subject, see my article "Ruptures in History," *Historically Speaking* vol. XII (3) (June 2011).

10.    Cf. Walter A. McDougall, *The Heavens and the Earth: A Political History of the Space Age* (New York: Basic Books, 1985).

11.    See *Globalinc. An Atlas of the Multinational Corporation* (New York: New Press, 2003), by Medard Gabel and Henry Bruner, a project of the New Global History Initiative/Toynbee Foundation.

12.    See, for example, Neva Goodwin et al. (2002).

13.    Alas, Africa tends to lag behind in terms of computer usage.

14.    See Bruce Mazlish, *The Idea of Humanity in a Global Era* (New York: Palgrave Macmillan, 2009).

15.    Quoted in Joan Acocella, "Blocked," *The New Yorker*, 6/14/04, 128. See Ian Hacking, *Historical Ontology* (Harvard University Press, 2002).

16. See William Easterly, "Foreign Aid for Scoundrels," *NYRB*, Nov. 25, 2010; Philip Gourevitch, "Alms Dealers," *The New Yorker*, 10/11/10; and Linda Polman, *War Games: The Story of Aid and War in Modern Times* (Viking, 2010).

17. John M. Headley, *The Europeanization of the World. On the Origins of Human Rights and Democracy* (Princeton University Press, 2008). Lynn Hunt, *Inventing Human Rights: A History* (W. W. Norton, 2007).

18. Kenneth Anderson, "Samuel Moyn on the History of the Human Rights Movement," *The Volokh Conspiracy*. http://www.volokh.com/2010/09/10/samuel-moyn-on-the-history-of-the-human-rights-movement.

19. Martin W. Lewis and Kären E. Wigen, *The Myth of Continents* (University of California Press, 1997).

# 10

# Social Bonding, Globalization, and Humanity*

In *The Descent of Man*, Darwin declares that "Man is a social being."[1] Being so gives the human species crucial survival advantages. As with other animals, such bonding allows them to hunt in packs and to warn one another of danger. It gives rise to feelings of love and of morality. Darwin further believes that such bonds arise from parental or filial feelings. The key is sympathy, which he calls "the all-important emotion." Indeed, he is not alone in his emphasis on sympathy. It is one of the most important subjects in the eighteenth and nineteenth centuries in Western Europe.[2] It is central, for example, in Adam Smith's *Theory of the Moral Sentiments*, which Darwin cites repeatedly. Sympathy is undoubtedly a key word in the thought of the time.

In the contemporary world we are told that "The hottest topic in brain research these days is social cognition; the unparalleled ability of humans to forge social bonds . . . embedded from birth in a rich and enriching skein of social relationships. . . . [W]e owe the very existence of our large brains to the need to keep track of the social whirl."[3]

Moreover, as a result of the inquiries of archaeologists and anthropologists, it appears that for 90–99 percent of its existence, the human species has been in hunter-gatherer groups, numbering between ten and forty to fifty members. Such groups foraged far and wide, being in touch with other such groups for pairings and occasional trade. Mainly, however, such groups, which I shall call bands, had social bonds only within the band. Eventually such bands, sometimes made up of a single family, united into a clan. Social bonds had been widened. In many ways, history can be told henceforth in the widening, and sometimes breakdown, of such bonds.

A key date seems to be the emergence of Cro-Magnon man (and the disappearance of Neanderthal man) about forty thousand years ago. Another key date is when members of the human species began to labor in agriculture, about twelve to fourteen thousand years ago, and with settled agriculture came the existence of towns. Bonding now extended from one's family members to other families. In a clan we witness the coming together of a number of households, whose heads claim descent from a common ancestor. (The Scottish Highlands serve as a good example.) Not all was always peaceful among clans (the fratricide of Cain and Abel is a recurrent theme). Nevertheless, the ties among families were extended, both in war and in peace.

When families, clans, and generations began to come together, they formed tribes. The persistence of this form of bonding is remarkable. Much of the history of medieval Europe consists of tribal invasions, often from the North but actually from all sides of the heartland. That heartland at the time could be described as the establishment by the Etruscans of a form of bonding that eventually became the Roman Empire. In China a centralized government was to be found. At the same time there existed as well a Persian Empire. The other development that requires recognition is the formation of city-states. One begins even to talk of civilizations.

The social bonding that takes place in the city, partly in the form of new kinds of interdependence, is of extraordinary importance. The city, while dependent on a rural hinterland for sustenance, allows for a degree of economic, cultural, and social exchange hitherto unknown. In its confines (and it is frequently surrounded by walls), social stratification arises. Specialization in military and priestly functions takes place. Merchants, tradespeople, and craftsmen appear, all dependent on one another. Intellectual life proliferates, and theater, with its own sites, can flourish. Numerous types of political forms can exist, ranging from Aztec-like monoliths to Greek-style agoras. In the latter, debates and discussions could abound, with philosophy often serving as a guide. The city could often be the center of political control, whether unto itself or as the place from which a kingdom or empire might be ruled. Not least of its functions was to administer taxation, a way of extracting the needed surplus from the peasantry. One can begin to speak of a bureaucracy in this regard.

In affinity with cities arose the idea of cosmopolitanism. This was the conviction, arising beyond the bonds of local and national ties, that one was a citizen of the world. Aligned with this view was the enormously fecund idea of all peoples and individuals bound together by their humanity. As Terence said in the second century AD, "Nothing human is alien to me." The social class carrying this message was most likely to be the merchants and philosophers. It was the ties created by economic exchange that began to make this notion real on the ground.

Especially from their polished cities, most social groups made a distinction between their own civilized behavior and that of the barbarians without. This gave rise to the notion of a civilizing process. Made most salient by the work of the German sociologist Norbert Elias, this process gave coherence to much of history. It also, late in time, was the inspiration for the reification of the term civilization. To us, who speak it so frequently, it has seemed omnipresent and long-standing. In fact, it was first used by Comte Mirabeau, the elder (his son was the great French Revolutionary orator) in 1756, in his book *L'Ami des Hommes*. A decade later it was in wide currency and is so still in the twenty-first century.[4]

Civilization is a loaded term. It came to dominate much of nineteenth-century international affairs. It served as part of Western imperialism, used as a justification for imposing their rule on lesser breeds, with the promise of leading them to the heights of civilization. It also served as the framework for establishing the international order: only those countries that had reached the refinement of civilization could take equal part. In a brilliant treatment, Gerrit Gong has shown how the system worked, and how eventually only Japan breached the Western institutionalization of the idea, with Japanese of both sexes learning Western ballroom dancing in the process.[5] It is also worth noting that before the Nuremberg trials and their crimes against humanity the phrase generally used was crimes against *civilization* and humanity.

Returning to our general account, the line leading from clans, tribes, and city-states to civilized kingdoms was a cliché in the writings of many Scottish enlightenment thinkers in the eighteenth century, such as Adam Ferguson and Adam Smith. The other major development in the West was the rise of nation-states. This institution arose as foraging and invading tribes from Northern Europe and other geographical zones settled down and eventually united into kingdoms. These entailed larger social bonds, especially extended by the growth of commerce, with populations gradually acquiring sentimental ties to a nation as an imagined community.[6]

The phrase is from Benedict Anderson, and his book on the origin and spread of nationalism. As he puts it, the nation "is *imagined* because the members of even the smallest nation will never know most of their fellow-members, meet them, or even hear of them, yet in the minds of each lives the image of their communion."[7] Obviously, this is not the case for clans, where face-to-face meeting is the norm.

Is the imagined community comparable to utopias? In most utopias, members usually are envisaged as living in harmony with one another. Communist society, once it gets rid of the bourgeoisie and establishes the dictatorship of the proletariat, is assumed to be completely peaceful. With the cash nexus overcome, only comradely ties are expected to exist. Alas, we know the reality of the Soviet Union, in which Marxism/Leninism realized itself. In literature dystopias appeared alongside of utopias to predict this result.

There is one other statement that Anderson makes that is highly relevant to our treatment of social bonding and Humanity. It is his comment that "No nation imagines itself coterminous with mankind."[8] The very notion of a nation-state requires the exclusion of others. The Italian nationalist, Giuseppe Garibaldi, might believe that his pursuit of nationalism in Italy would lead to the broader concept of Humanity, but subsequent events hardly have borne out his optimism. Nation-state ties are quite a stretch as it is; indeed, in many of the 192 nation-states belonging to the UN, many, if not most, have tribal alliances that threaten the unitary nature of the state. We must give true acknowledgment to the strains involved in the broadening of bonds from the tribe to the state, and thus be more fully aware of the obstacles to its further broadening to Humanity.

We must also consider the issue of territory. Deeply embedded in the human makeup, the issue of territory emerged after hunter-gatherers began to settle down. Its major expression in the past three hundred years or so has been in the form of the nation-state. One of the nation-state's prominent manifestations is in terms of lines drawn on a map. This is its territory, justifying an army to defend it, and a strong, centralized government to preserve its integrity. Where, in this context, can we find the territory of Humanity? From outer space, one sees the blue planet without territorial lines upon it. This, then, is the domain of Humanity. Most people, it must be acknowledged, do not live in outer space. On Earth, one can put up frontiers. And require passports. Humanity cannot be so demarcated.

Akin to imagined communities, but ontologically different, is the notion of society. It emerged from a growing reality and signifies an evolving consciousness as to a form of human bonding. This seems to have taken place somewhere between the end of the sixteenth and beginning of the seventeenth century in Western Europe. Some assign a later date, placing it in the eighteenth century. Its firm use is evident in Thomas Carlyle's proclaiming in 1833 the existence of "industrial society" as marking a break with "feudal society."

The term *society* is one of the keywords in Raymond William's book *Keywords*. In a second edition, which I read, I was forced to revise my original favorable impression. The book is simply a version of sorts of the *Oxford English Dictionary*. (The same can be said, more or less, of *New Keywords*, ed. by Tony Bennett et al., Blackwell). It is William's *Culture & Society 1780–1950* that remains praiseworthy, as well as his *The Country and the City*.

One way to define society is as the space between state and religious institutions. The notion of society implies, or pointedly announces, that the human bonding to be found in society is not god-given, but realizes itself in the day-to-day relations of human beings. It is their social construct. And as such, it is subject to change and even to what can be seen as progress. Much of that progress can be found in the realms of science and technology. Equally, however, it can emerge from the discourse of what came to be called civil society. Present, for example, in prerevolutionary eighteenth-century France, this part of society was composed mainly of the growing bourgeoisie and enlightened aristocrats.[9]

At about this time emerged the social sciences as disciplines. These, whether economics, sociology, or history were to serve as guides to consciously bringing about progress. One pioneer was Adam Smith, who showed how society was constructed on the basis of the division of labor, and how self-interest turned out to benefit mankind as much as did benevolence. With Auguste Comte the science of sociology entered the scene, to explain those areas of life overlooked or neglected by economics. As a result of such efforts, the relations of human beings appeared amenable to analysis and even control.[10]

With these achievements in mind, we can now go back in time in our effort to give a historical background to the subject of social bonding. Let us turn to the Middle East, where from the seventh century on, with the coming of Mohammad, the religion of Islam spread quickly and widely. Muslims conquered the Sasanid (Persian) Empire and controlled the North African and Syrian territories of the Byzantine Empire. Inhabitants of the desert as well as the city became connected as a result, unified by the Arabic language, which like Latin in the Middle Ages, only more so, became a common tongue. Muslim empires rose and fell, but Islam itself consistently expanded. As we are told, "In contrast to tribal groups, the new community, or *unmah*, was open to anyone who made the basic affirmation of faith, and loyalty to the unmah was to supersede any other loyalty, whether to clan, family, or commercial partnership."[11]

Without going into further details, it is clear that both in the East and the West, significant expansion of social bonding had taken place over many centuries. Whereas the Jewish religion restricted itself to the Chosen People and made no effort to convert others, the other great monotheistic religions, of Christianity and Islam, were expansive, and made leaps and bounds in tying peoples together. At the same time, they had their limits: who is not with me is my enemy. The fierce Christian-Muslim conflicts of the Middle Ages is evidence of this fact (not to mention the horrible intra-Christian violence). Thus, there was a barrier to pushing social bonding to include all of humanity.

It should be noted before going on that bonding could be to more than one group. In the words of the philosopher and sociologist Dmitri Shalin, "A modern individual belongs to several groups at once, each one furnishing a different perspective on reality. It is on [sic] the intersection of such publicly defined perspectives that we discover what reality is, and this reality is bound to be multiple, pluralistic, tinged with uncertainty, and open to conflicting interpretations."[12] Social bonding, in other words, while inviting harmony, may be filled with tensions and divergent pulls. New bonds can be created and old ones broken with some frequency.

The story of Antigone is one such dramatic illustration of this fact. As Sophocles's tragedy unfolds, Antigone must decide which tie is greater, that to her family or that to the king. In the play, Antigone's dilemma resounds through the ages. It is a classic one. As she responds to Cleon, "Nowise from Zeus, methought, this edict came, / Nor Justice, that abides among the gods / In Hades, who ordained these laws for men. / Nor did I deem *thine* edicts of such force / That they, a mortal's bidding, should o'erride / Unwritten laws, eternal in the heavens. / Not of to-day or yesterday are these, / But live from everlasting, and from whence / They sprang, none knoweth."[13] This appeal to a higher tie is found in many religions and adherents of conscience.

Let us resume our brief historical account. In the past, for example, as in the Christian Middle Ages, poor transportation hindered widened ties. Roads were sparse, and travel on them where they existed was difficult at the best of times. Trade was hampered by the motley weights and measures that were applied to them. These obstacles hindered "exchange." This is a key term in the writing of Georg Simmel, the great German sociologist.[14] Further, coinage, that great lubricant of economic exchange, was in short supply. Given the limitations of the market in a basically subsistence society, division of labor would have to wait a few centuries before making itself known to the discerning eye of Adam Smith. The social bonding facilitated by Christianity was now more and more supplemented, if not replaced, by what came to be called the cash nexus. Denounced by Karl Marx, changed more and more into the intangibility of credit, it linked people together in a mysterious but extensive way.

We can also turn to Karl Marx for his prescient view that capitalism was turning the world into a single market, and compelling all to enter into it. Marx, along with many others, was aware that the Age of Discovery was a signal event, revealing an entire new world, one linked with what one might describe as silver (coinage) ties. This event, along with the Portuguese venture into Asia, marked the advent of European imperialism, which dominated so much of the centuries that followed. This was characterized by colonialism, which witnessed the planting of European rule in new territories. Here, again, we see the presence of expanding social bonds.

I have written this thumbnail sketch of past social bonding in order to set the stage, although with little scenery, for inquiry into more contemporary happenings. The most important of these is the emergence after World War II of the process of globalization. It is truly a rupture in human history.[15] Its core definition is increased interdependence and interconnectedness. The process has been going on, as I have tried to show, all through history. It is only after World War II that it takes on unprecedented impulse. The coining and currency of the term globalization in the 1950s through the 1980s is one piece of evidence. While much involved with economic expansion it is, in my view, preeminently the development of global *consciousness* that will ultimately be of the greatest importance.

The seeing revolution, the computer revolution, and globalization are leading toward a new concept of Humanity. Such a concept implies a loyalty and identity that transcends, while including, more local attachments, such as to a nation-state. It begins, in fact, to take on sovereign force, although as yet only in vague and weak form. Its future power lies ahead of it.[16] Such power can be facilitated. A logo, for example, comparable to that for the UN, would give visible evidence of Humanity's presence. Rituals need to be devised—comparable to Earth Day. Perhaps even monuments and statuary need to be created. A website can help establish a virtual community, worldwide, and provide an agora for people everywhere to further analyze the concept of Humanity and exchange views on its nature. Such a website could also facilitate the sharing of views as to how best to foster the dissemination of the idea.

It is worth noting another way in which people establish common ties. They bind their identities to an athletic team. For example, in 2011, the Boston hockey team defeated the team from Vancouver to win the Stanley Cup. The fans of the Bruins as they were called were riotously happy, holding a parade through downtown Boston, where their heroes stood in cars acknowledging their fans' delirium. Less inspiring on the other hand, the supporters of the defeated Vancouver team expressed their rage by rampaging through the streets of that town, overturning cars and breaking store windows.

What we have here is identification with a team, which, acted on by many people, establishes a powerful tie. Supporters of each team acknowledge similar supporters and are joined together. It can be seen as a form of totem worship—notice the use of animals such as Bruins or the Detroit Lions, a football team; we could also add the Columbia Lions. Just as the totem carvings of an animal symbolize the social bonding of a clan, these namings allow people to come together. Indeed, it can go well beyond the immediate clan and include strangers. We are all familiar with the phenomenon of complete strangers nodding to each other and saying, "We did well, didn't we?"

Let us return from these homey examples to our concept of Humanity. The future of Humanity as a desired form of social bonding is not determined, its path not yet clearly laid out. All of human actions are infused with contingency. What humans can try to do is to stick a paddle in the currents pushing it hither and yon. The efforts toward greater Humanity are facilitated by a number of features. Globalization has already been stressed. Another favoring factor is what the philosopher Ian Hacking has called "dynamic nominalism." Humanity is an example of such a contemporary dynamic nominalism.

More is needed. It comes, I believe, from the challenges to Humanity that are presented by such global happenings as climate change and the ecological devastation caused by rapacious exploitation of the earth's resources. These happenings are, of course, contentious: so is Darwin's theory of evolution. As in all such matters, it is a question of the weight and quality of the arguments that count. The morality, as well as best knowledge, involved in Humanity must be brought to bear so that human evolution, cultural now rather than physical, can go forward in a way that this thinking as well as feeling species can regard with a sense of grandeur, as well as humility.

# Notes

\*   I would like to acknowledge the critical reading of this article by Neva Goodwin and Kenneth Weisbrode.

1.   Charles Darwin, *The Origin of Species and The Descent of Man* (The Modern Library, nd.), 480.

2.   See further Bruce Mazlish, *A New Science. The Breakdown of Connections and the Birth of Sociology* (Oxford, 1989; paper ed. Penn State University Press, 1993), 15-18.

3.   htttp://www.pbs.org/wnet/humanspark/episodes/program-three/introduction/23.

4.   See Bruce Mazlish, *Globalization and Its Contents* (Stanford University Press, 2004).

5.   Gerrit W. Gong, *The Standard of 'Civilization' in International Society* (Oxford University Press, 1984).

6.   For a detailed account, see Jacques LeGoff, *Medieval Civilisation. 400-1500,* tr. Julia Barrow (London, 2011; first pub. In French, 1964).

7.   Benedict Anderson, *Imagined Communities: Reflections on the Origin and Spread of Nationalism* (London: Verso, 1983+1989), 15.

8.   Ibid., 16.

9.   For a magisterial treatment of civil society, see Jean L. Cohen and Andrew Arato, *Civil Society and Political Theory* (MIT Press, 1992).

10.  For this and more, see Bruce Mazlish, *A New Science. The Breakdown of Connections & the Birth of Sociology* (Oxford, 1989).

11.  From *Encyclopedia of Politics and Religion,* ed. Robert Wuthnow. 2 vols. (Washington, DC: Congressional Quarterly, Inc., 1998), 383-393. For one of the early Western efforts to understand Islam and its society, in their own terms, see Marshall G. S. Hodgson, *The Venture of Islam,* 3 vols. (University of Chicago Press, 1974).

12.  Dmitri N. Shalin, *Pragmatism & Democracy* (Transaction Publishers, 2011), 250.

13.  C. A. Robinson Jr. (ed.) *An Anthology of Greek Drama* (Rinehart Editions, New York, 1950), 115.

14. See Georg Simmel, *The Philosophy of Money* (Routledge, 1978).
15. For the meaning and proper use of the term "rupture," see "Ruptures in History," Note 9. in Ch. 9.
16. Cf. Bruce Mazlish, *The Idea of Humanity in a Global Era* (Palgrave, 2009).

# Conclusion

What is the significance of the transition from modernity to globalization? Some of the answers will undoubtedly unfold as more time passes. I will try to deal here with a few of the significant ones now discernible, recognizing that others exist, either now or in the future.

Among the most significant and perhaps subtle is the shift in the categories of thought. By these I mean the fundamental ways in which we think. For example, there is a vast difference between pre- and post-Copernican conceptions of the universe. Just as great is the pre- and post-Darwinian picture of time and the evolution of the human species.

In modernity the overarching canopy has been that of nation-states and the international system erected to order their relations. The very word inter-*national* is key to what is involved. Coined by Jeremy Bentham in the early nineteenth century, it fitted the times and gave meaning to the existing system. Essential to the nation-state concept has been the notion of sovereignty, which is seen by nationalists as inviolable.

With globalization, the nation-state is still central in many ways. Yet, with so many of humanity's current problems global in nature, the nation-state has proven too often to be a constrictive force, unable to cope adequately with its challenges. Indeed, the very notion of territory and fixed boundaries can appear anachronistic in a globalizing era.

When planet Earth is viewed from outer space, such lines disappear. As Lewis and Wigen capture the new situation; in their geography the nation-state lines on the map fade away. Such depiction matches the increasing de-territoralization of institutions in the global era.

One result of this development is that new players have appeared on the scene: multinational corporations whose operations and influence are worldwide; nongovernmental organizations that live in uneasy relation to the nation-state, assuming many of its tasks while also challenging its boundaries; the United Nations, which is in principle the pinnacle of international justice and peace; and lastly the juridical system, which, starting from the Nuremberg Trials of 1945–46, followed by the Yugoslavia and Rwanda trials, has eventuated in the International Criminal Court.

Another consequence for social scientists is to make us rethink the subject of archives. For the last century and a half they have been the bedrock of historical inquiry. A doctoral student's discovery of a new archive could bring forth much rewriting of received texts. In regard to modernity, these were *national* archives. How do we conceive of archives in a global era? The subject requires creative new thinking—especially in a time in which a computer revolution has been and is taking place.

Developments such as these have changed the ways in which we think of the political, social, and cultural world— our categories of thought. The core of modernity—the Enlightenment—is being rethought in global terms. In a pioneering article, Sebastian Conrad has shown us how limited and Eurocentric our treatments of the subject have been up to now.[1] In the light of such work, the nation-state is increasingly on its way to taking second place on the global stage.

(2)

Another important result is in regard to identity. Is there such a thing as global identity? Identity is a protean concept. When Sigmund Freud speaks of "identification with the aggressor" we find it easy to understand what he means. A child afraid of a lion goes roaring around the room, screaming, "I am a lion." In the Stockholm experience we can comprehend why the hostage placates its taker by embracing his feelings.

The *concept* of identity itself is much more complicated. Building on Freud's work the lay analyst Erik Erikson discerned what he called an "identity crisis." It usually occurred around the time of adolescence but was potential at other times as well. The person asks "Who am I?" The answer is almost always plural. We all have multiple identities, and a problem is how to rank them.

Names can figure hugely. When Cassius Clay changed his name to Mohammed Ali, he was signifying a shift from an identity in which he was named after a slave owner to one whereby he asserted a new self as a Muslim. Erikson's case is also interesting. Raised by his stepfather, a Dr. Hamburger, Erikson chose to give up that name and named himself, Erik, son of Erik. Thus, he opted for a new identity in which he connected to a Danish and Christian link, in fact to an unknown father (Erikson's mother was Jewish, as was Dr. Hamburger).

A pressing problem is often how to transcend local identities that lead to violent conflict and provide people with a larger one that can end such animosities. A poignant example has been the Hutu massacre—genocide—of Tutsis in Rwanda. Even though there were frequent intermarriages (the same was the case in Nazi Germany), the two groups thought of themselves as separate and opposed. Only by thinking of themselves as Rwandans could they truly transcend their differences in a peaceful manner. It is a story repeated in many countries. It is also a story of how peoples, say, Rwandans, need now to add to their national identity a global one.

Let us also reflect on what Freud called "the narcissism of small differences." As has been remarked, small variations can produce more rage than large ones because they put identity into question. Thus, Socialists and Communists have been bitter enemies, even though they share much in common—or rather because they have so much in common. The same can be said, for example, about Communist parties in various countries. Identity, as remarked earlier, is a complex, multilayered matter.

At the moment global identity may be largely a question of generations. One scholar, Julia Docolas at Leipzig, on the basis of her preliminary research, suggests that her generation, say, 15 to 35 years of age, is the first to see themselves in common as a digital generation. Using a group of about 145 students from all over the world in a program at Leipzig dedicated to global studies, Docolas studies them as empirical evidence for her thesis. Others have called them Generation Y.

Such a thesis might help explain, and be corroborated by, the so-called April uprisings that have been recently occurring in the Middle East. Here, in fact, is a promising research project. We must remember that the age group of about twenty-five to thirty-five has almost always been at the forefront of revolutions, since that of 1789. It appears that the Internet offers such a group increased means to promote mass uprisings.

In various of the chapters on globalization I inquired into the concept of Humanity. It can in the present context be thought of as an emergent identity. In addition, say, to my being Chinese, European or American, I am human, an identification that adds to and transcends my more local identifications. As I have argued in some of the previous chapters, the emergence of an identification with Humanity is increasingly a result of globalization, with its increased inter-connectivity and increased interdependency, allowing more and more people to have shared experiences, values, and a sense of oneness. This tendency is also fostered by dynamic nominalism, whereby a newly created category comes to be filled by real people.

Norbert Elias, the great German sociologist, offers us a mechanism by which this process might unfold. Emphasizing how integration into larger coordinated units is fostered by violent encounters of peoples, he argues that the overall trend has been toward survival units larger and larger both in population and geographical extent.[2]

Others, I hope, will give thought and will work actively to make Humanity more and more a visible presence and a new kind of sovereignty. Naturally, there are all sorts of problems in bringing the idea of humanity down from the clouds and actively moving forward on the ground. For example, for Elias violence has been the essential lever in moving societies to greater integration. It is not a tool Humanity is keen to turn to. Yet wars have been a mechanism for postwar advances toward international justice. How do we reconcile this fact with the intrinsic opposition of the concept of Humanity to war? In many ways, to answer this question is the challenge of the new digital generation.

(3)

My short list will conclude with a few reflections. The first is in regard to hierarchy. Much of modernity can be thought of as an effort to combat hierarchy and promote equality. In this centuries-long development, globalization can be viewed as a powerful force also fostering equality. Everyone, supposedly, speaks with an equal voice on the Internet.

This is partly so, but the greater reality is that the rich have gotten richer and the poor poorer. Such is the case within societies and between societies. One understands the pull of

Thomas Friedman's idea that the world is becoming flat. Alas, looked at more closely, in the light of the disparity between wealth and power among peoples and nations, the notion itself becomes flat.

The concept of hierarchical leveling is relevant in regard to horizontal communication. Whether this horizontal communication can allow masses of people to be in touch with one another and to organize in such a fashion as to level much of the inequality that continues to exist is a leading question. It is one which only the further unrolling and study of globalization will be able to answer.

My concluding reflection is that like the satellites and spacecraft spun into the heavens, I have been soaring high above the events of the present day. Here, China is emerging as a dynamic global power. The US and the West remain powerful economic and military forces. The pressing problem of today is to make sure that these two remain friendly competitors, not arrogant opponents. Even above this specific necessity is the need to balance the forces of universalism and particularity, unity and diversity, community and individual freedom, integration and autonomy in our world. This, surely, is a worthwhile task for present and future generations.

## Notes

1.    Sebastian Conrad, "Enlightenment in Global History: A Historiographical Critique," *The American Historical Review*, vol. 117 (4), October 2012, 999–1027.
2.    See Norbert Elias's *On the Process of Civilisation, The Collected Works of Norbert Elias, vol. 3* (2012). This has been superbly edited by Stephen Mennell.

# Index